THE GLORY OF GOD REVEALED

DONNA RIGNEY

Donna Rigney

It's Supernatural! Press and Messianic Vision Inc.

Cover and interior design by Terry Clifton

ISBN 13 TP: 978-0-7684-6125-1
ISBN 13 eBook: 978-0-7684-6126-8
ISBN 13 HC: 978-0-7684-6128-2
ISBN 13 LP: 978-0-7684-6127-5

For Worldwide Distribution, Printed in the U.S.A.
2 3 4 5 6 7 8 / 25 24 23 22 21

DEDICATION

In deep gratitude to my faithful, loving Father, to my kind and gentle Savior and Friend, Jesus, and to wonderful Holy Spirit, who has helped me to know, love and serve God, I dedicate this work to the awesome Trinity.

I saw the glory of the God of Israel coming from the east. His voice was like the roar of rushing waters, and the land was radiant with his glory.

—Ezekiel 43:1-2

CONTENTS

Introduction

The Commission Given

For I know the plans I have for you," declares the Lord, "plans to prosper you and not to harm you, plans to give you hope and a future.

—Jeremiah 29:11

As was my custom, I went to my prayer room one sunny morning and sat down in my comfortable chair, turned my worship music on and worshiped my Father. Little did I know, this day would mark a tremendous change in my life. It was not uncommon for me to hear my Lord speak, nor was it unusual for me to see Him appear before me. Frequently, Holy Spirit took me in the spirit to see those things my natural eyes couldn't see.

In the past, I had been taken in the spirit many times to visit Heaven and Hell. Other days the Holy Spirit brought me to visit with Father and Jesus on the top of a very high mountain that overlooks this world. I came to know this mountain as the mountain of intimacy. There is a comfortable bench at the very top of this mountain that overlooks the world. Sitting on this seat between

Father and Jesus, I was often shown, in graphic visions, events which would be coming to the world and to my nation.

This day I was not taken to visit Heaven or to Hell, nor was I brought to the mountain of intimacy; instead, the Father came to visit me. Alone in my room, just like the Lord spoke to Jeremiah, in Jeremiah 1:11, I heard Him say: "What do you see!"

I looked with my spiritual eyes into the spirit realm, and I saw a large hand. This hand was strong and enormous but gentle—a hand I could trust. This hand was bigger than I was; it covered me completely. Then I saw His face look right at me. I couldn't escape His look, nor did I want to. I felt like a tiny creature being looked at by a massive giant. His face was not clearly visible, but I felt the warmth of His smile.

Very gently, He picked me up and put me on His strong, broad shoulder saying, "Daughter, don't forget that I am a big God. You have won My heart, and I do approve of you. Faith can allow you to sit right here on My shoulder, continually, where you have access to My heart and My ear. Believe that I am a big God, with the heart of a gentle, but mighty, wise Father, who will do anything to protect and to provide for My little children that I adore."

Building my faith stronger in who He is, my Father continued: "I have already overcome all the powers of darkness, so it is easy for Me to carry the weight of this world on My shoulders. Never forget how big I am! Only your sight of Me will limit Me from doing the wonders I plan on doing in this hour. See Me as I am, and I will never be limited by your unbelief, when you pray.

"I am the God who easily does the impossible, who speaks to nothing and worlds are created, who creates body parts for those who lose theirs, and who longs for the love and companionship of My children. I am the God who does everything out of love. Place all your trust in Me, and you will see miracles. You will never be disappointed, as you pray with faith for My will to be done, because My will is to bless and prosper you, to give you a hope and a future!"

After encouraging me and building my faith with His wise counsel, to my surprise, He exclaimed: "I want you to be My messenger to this world. Many wonder what I think and what I say, but very few are devoted enough to Me, to take the time to sit with Me daily to develop a true relationship with Me, and to learn to see and to hear what I am saying. You have paid the price to know, to see, to hear, to receive and to adore. Now We say, 'Tell all; yes, tell all that We have spoken and shown you.' Many hearts will be set ablaze with a fiery love for Us, as they encounter Us through your revelations. Then We will draw them away with Us in intimate communion and show them the wonders We have shown you."

In awe of His majesty and humbled by His call, I agreed to allow Him to use me to proclaim His words and share the revelations He has given me.

Recommissioned by My Father

A short time later, while in prayer, Holy Spirit brought me to visit Heaven where Father once again repeated His commission. Looking into the spirit, to my delight, I saw myself walking with my Father through His lush garden in Heaven. Father reached out and picked a flower and gave it to me to take back to the Earth when I returned, saying:

"This is what I want you to do. Come into the heavenly realm and receive revelations from My heart. Then take those revelations and present them to My people on My behalf. Bring to each a flower, or to some even a bouquet. After you give them My truth and leave them, I remain in that revelation. I will continue to nourish and strengthen them through the sweet-smelling savor of the blossoms of truth. I will frequently remind them to come and drink deeply, as they partake of the fragrance again and again.

"When you have completed your work of bringing My message, I am just beginning to work on their behalf. Each revelation you share, imparts the life and love from Heaven into their lives. Do not hesitate to bring those truths, for they are life to their souls and healing to their minds and bodies. Faith comes by hearing. Who can receive more faith, if no one will speak My words and deliver My fragrant blossoms of truth?"

Bolstering my confidence, He declared, "Don't hold back for fear of being rejected. For I will confirm your words continually, and they will know that a prophet has come among them."

In obedience to my God and dear Friend Who commissioned me to bring His words to His children, I am sharing these wonderful visitations. Many of these awesome revelations detail what I saw of the wonders Heaven holds for us in a very special place He has built for us there called the Mountain of Glory. Others are accounts of truths He taught me, and instructed me to pass on to His children while we sat together on the mountain of intimacy. Numerous times, while in prayer, He brought me in the spirit and revealed future events coming to our world and the USA.

During all of these visitations, I dutifully recorded what I saw and heard. Not only are these words filled with wisdom and revelations of the future, they reveal the heart of God towards His children.

> *... It seemed good also to me to write in orderly account for you... I have been sent to speak to you and to tell you this good news* (Luke 1: 3,19).

You, too, Can Access His Glory

Before you begin *The Glory of God Revealed* and come with me on this journey of heavenly revelation, I would like to explain how easy it is for everyone to develop a delightful friendship with our God. Many people have asked me how they, too, can encounter the glory of God. It is not a select few that He has called to know Him and to spend time in sweet fellowship with Him; He calls all of His children to intentionally set time to be apart with Him.

Soon after I was saved and surrendered my life to Jesus, I felt a tug at my heart to get to know the Lord. I deeply desired to hear Him speak to me. These are the steps Holy Spirit led me to take to develop that close friendship I longed to have.

I first made a conscious decision to spend time daily with the Holy Spirit who dwells in us. This was not always easy, because many distractions seemed to draw me away from my resolution. To help me implement my plan, I felt led to get my calendar and set aside a special time that was reserved just for Him. In order to do this, I decided to think of my time with the Lord like a very special appointment that could not be broken. All doctors' visits, phone calls and shopping trips were scheduled after my prayer time was complete. I made sure that I allowed sufficient time for our daily visits and didn't take phone calls or allow any interruptions. I realized that this type of discipline is essential to having a special bond with the Lord.

Very quickly I learned that entering into my Lord's presence was much easier if I played soft worship music. The songs that helped me feel His nearness became the ones at the top of my list. I purchased a headset and CD player and when I sat down in my spot away from everyone else, I immediately played my music. Once I quieted myself and began to worship from my heart, His loving presence always came upon me.

Daily I spent my time alone with Jesus worshiping and interceding for those things and people I felt led to pray for, and then I read my Bible for a while. Because my longing for Him was so intense, I made a decision to never leave my time of prayer unless I heard from my Friend. When something I was reading in Scripture touched my heart, I knew I was hearing Holy Spirit speak directly to me through those words.

Frustrated that my time alone wasn't producing the ability to hear my Lord clearly, other than through the Scriptures, I sought Holy Spirit daily asking Him to please let me hear Him speak. After months of seeking Him faithfully, I learned that the Holy Spirit was talking to me, but my mind was having a hard time being still enough to hear Him speak. To my delight, He taught me a trick that I use to this day.

After I sit before Him and worship, basking in His presence, I listen for what words or thoughts come to my mind, and I write them down in a notebook. No matter what I hear within me, I write it down. I found that this practice of listening and writing what I am hearing quiets my mind enough to hear Holy Spirit speak—not just a few words, but for a longer length of time, without being distracted. While concentrating on what I am writing, like a flow, the words keep pouring forth from within. To focus on what I am writing and hearing truly helps to keep my mind from wandering.

Once I feel like my Lord has finished talking to me in this way, I always ask for Him to confirm His words to me through a Scripture. Then I open my Bible wherever I feel led and read the verses. I do this so that I am confident that I am hearing Him and not just listening to my own thoughts. Without fail, Holy Spirit always confirms that I heard Him speaking by repeating the same message through the Scriptures. After years of daily worshiping, listening, writing and reading the Scripture that confirms His word to me, I have learned to clearly discern His voice.

Through practicing this daily discipline, I have become very devoted to my Lord. Spending time getting to know Him only makes me love Him more. He is altogether lovely! Devotion to Him is essential to experiencing His best—His glory.

Encountering His Glory Described

Before the glory manifested in my life, I often felt the anointing fall on me in my times with Jesus. This anointing felt like His love was pouring out on me. During these wonderful experiences, I always felt loved, accepted and understood.

The difference between experiencing the anointing and encountering His glory is the level of intensity of His presence. In the glory, it feels like the anointing is greatly magnified. Instead of feeling like I have a coating of His love on me, I feel like a large bucket of His love as His power and His presence is poured out all over my being. A feeling of being undone—or almost being incapacitated—comes while His glory rests on me. His breath becomes mine! Our hearts beat as one!

In both encounters—those while under the anointing and those under the glory—I am able to hear Holy Spirit, Father and Jesus speak to me. While under the glory, His words are clearer,

His presence dearer and His equipping stronger. Tears of devotion flow down my face unabated, while my heart expands with His overwhelming love. All negative feelings flee while His glory is present. Worries, fearful thoughts, even pains in my body disappear when I am encountering His glory. His glory makes all my burdens light. Faith for the prayers I am praying is suddenly stronger; love for the unlovable comes pouring on me; visitations in the spirit are easily accessible; deep revelations feel like they come directly from His heart to mine. When the glory is upon me, it feels like my heart is joined with His.

In the glory worship just happens. There is no effort involved. Wisdom is imparted in the glory. His glory resides in His embracing arms. His greatest reward is His glory pouring out on his devoted children. He invites all to come and sit with Him and receive His glory.

Resting in His Glory

A good friend of mine recently had a very impacting dream that very clearly explains the manifestation of the glory of God. In this supernatural dream, she saw herself sleeping in her bed. While she was sleeping she was praying in tongues, and as she prayed, gold dust poured forth from her mouth. The Holy Spirit was on her right side, and a seven foot tall angel was on her left side. It was evident to her that this massive angel was waiting for her prayers, so he could go implement them. As the dream progressed, she observed herself sitting between her two young daughters. Both of them were covered in a golden light. The glory was on them as well.

Through this inspiring dream, it was clear that God was showing her the power of resting in His glory. Her prayers, which were led by Holy Spirit standing beside her, were so powerful that angels were waiting to get them answered quickly. Even her family was impacted by His glory as she just stayed in His presence.

In many of my visitations, the Lord has encouraged me to soak in His glory. He has explained that when we get apart with Him and just spend quality time alone enjoying His presence, we are literally marinating in His goodness. If we marinate a piece of meat for a period of time before we cook it, it will end up having the flavor of the marinade in it. It is the same with us. If we marinate in the glory, we will have the flavor of God—His goodness and love—in us.

Once His glory comes on me in my time alone with Him, I just rest in it. Like in the dream my friend shared she was asleep, or simply resting, and God was doing great and wonderful things. To linger in His presence, or to spend time enjoying His love, will produce the character of Jesus in us. When His glory falls on me, I linger with Him until it lifts. I want all I can get from Him!

During these special times apart with my Friend, He has frequently brought me away with Him in the spirit and shown me wonderful things. This He will do for anyone who will hunger for Him enough to seek Him. Those who discipline themselves in this way will grow in their devotion, just as I did, and will enter the place in the spirit where He reveals Himself—His glory! His glory cannot be separated from Him; it is His essence.

Remember, as you read the pages of *The Glory of God Revealed,* when you hear His beckoning call to you to soak, or to spend time and linger in His glory, believe that it is very easy to do. He spoke this promise to me for you:

"Faith will arise in each one, as they take the first step to answer Our invitation to draw close to Us. That faith will be exercised each time they meet with Us, and it will grow daily as they draw near."

> *And we, who with unveiled faces all reflect the Lord's glory, are being transformed into his likeness with ever increasing glory, which comes from the Lord, who is the Spirit* (2 Corinthians 3:18).

HIS GLORY DISPLAYED ON THE MOUNTAIN OF GLORY

Come, let us go up to the mountain of the Lord, to the house of the God of Jacob. He will teach us his ways… For the Lord Almighty has spoken….

—Micah 4:1-5

Chapter One

The Wonders of His Glory Revealed

I have appeared to you to appoint you as a servant and as a witness of what you have seen of me and what I will show you.

—Acts 26:16

Frequently, as I sat daily visiting with Holy Spirit, Father and Jesus, I would be invited to go in the spirit to see and hear what They wanted to tell me and to show me. On one of these occasions, Jesus came to me in my prayer room and asked me to follow Him, in the spirit, to a magnificent place in Heaven. With no hesitation, I entered the spirit realm and followed Jesus as He lovingly brought me to the base of a gold mountain. I had seen many wonderful, even glorious things, on other encounters and visits to Heaven, but this one far exceeded what I had observed in the past.

Knowing that all of Heaven is filled with the love of God, I immediately knelt down and pressed my check against the gold path I had been standing on. Just as I expected, love poured out from this mountain into me. Jesus laughed and encouraged me to continue climbing beside Him.

As we walked together up this mountain made totally of gold, my Friend gave me a pair of sunglasses, because my earthly eyes were unable to handle the shimmering brightness of the dazzling brilliance of the gold. We laughed together and continued climbing this majestic gold mountain, high into the sky.

He instructed me, "Think of this mountain when the darkness on the Earth begins to overwhelm you; it is a reality in My kingdom. Think of those things I have shown you today and in the past, and that will diminish the sight of those things that are filled with darkness, and then your joy will be full.

"Think of the children at play in Heaven; think of the animals basking in the light of My glory and love; think of the flower gardens and the wheat fields that talk and sing, declaring My wonders. Think of your home and Mine. I have shown you many wonders that few have been privileged to see. Think about these visitations and all else will diminish in your sight.

"Teach My children, when they go through trials, to think about the wonders I have shown them and of the many good gifts I have showered upon them. It is a far better way that I am showing you today than to make mountains out of problems. Make mountains out of My glory and My majesty, then your peace and joy will return.

"When you are enduring trials or hearing about difficulties others are coping with, let Me bring you into the spirit to show you things that will distract you from those earthly issues at hand. Trust Me to show you daily what you need to see, and to speak to you that which will fill your heart with the richest of fare."

Entering the Garden of Glory

Then my Lord led me to a plateau on the side of His golden mountain. The most magnificent garden was hidden there. It had a dazzling white picket fence at its entrance. Together we walked through the open gate, and what I beheld was something I will never forget. Flowers of every kind were growing in this mammoth garden. The flowers and plants were giant-many times larger than any on the Earth. Most of the blossoms were about three feet in diameter.

Pondering how plants could grow in gold, my Lord explained: "If your flowers on Earth grow beautifully in soil, how much better do Mine grow here in My glory? My glory causes everything that soaks in it to grow, to display My wonders. As My garden plants soak in My glory and are nourished continually by My glory, you do the same. Soak in My glory, stay here continually in the place of the awareness of My goodness, and you and your gifts will bloom and grow, just like these flowers about you."

I saw enormous sunflowers that looked like they were smiling down at Jesus. Because they were so big, they towered over us. Elegant roses, of every color, showered us with their fragrance. I saw miles of multicolored plants blooming in the dazzling sunlight. Enormous daisies, daffodils, gladioli, and so many other flowers I didn't recognize from the Earth, greeted us.

I kept telling Jesus over and over, "It is so beautiful here; it is so beautiful here!" He just laughed at my delight: "You, and those who love My glory, can come here anytime. All are welcome to visit My garden on the Mountain of Glory."

Looking about, I could see a beautiful, golden garden swing. "Come sit and swing beside me and enjoy My glory. I will take care of all that concerns you on the Earth as we swing together. Keep your attention fixed on all that My glory provides."

Just one invitation was all I needed; I ran over to this magnificent, golden swing immersed in majestic flowers and sat beside my Lord. Hugged by His strong, kind arms, I was lost in His love. He told me that I could come to this place anytime; there are no limitations here in His kingdom. Plants can grow in gold here!

He said lovingly, "Nothing limits us here; this is the place where miracles are a way of life. If you need miracles, soak in My glory where all limitations are removed."

Spending Time in the Glory

A few weeks later, while sitting alone with my Friend, I saw myself in the spirit in the garden of glory sitting on the golden swing between Father and Jesus. The magnificent apple tree that grew in front of the inviting swing caught my attention. It was bigger—much bigger—than I remembered from my previous visit. Instantly I got off the swing and ran over to the large tree and hugged its enormous trunk.

Father and Jesus were standing beside me laughing. Getting my full attention, They pointed to the large branches of this magnificent tree. Looking up, I was completely amazed when I saw how large the fruit was that hung from its branches. These brilliant red apples were so big; one could easily feed many people. Father leaned over and told me that all the fruit that grows in the garden of glory feeds everyone in Heaven.

Then I heard: "Taste and see how good your God is. Yes, the essence of My being—My glory—fills the fruit here. The more everything soaks in My glory, the more of My goodness and My being permeates that fruit. As My children spend time soaking in My glory, the more of Me they will house in them. The fruit that pours forth from their lives will be like this fruit you are seeing grow here. The fruit of love, joy, peace, patience, kindness, goodness, faithfulness, gentleness and self-control will be enormous in their lives, too. The fruit of a life lived for, by, and with Me will be delicious and will nourish all they encounter. All deeds done by those who soak in My glory will be motivated by love. Selfishness will die and selfless love will prevail, for those who listen and obey My call to get apart with Me. Many who spend quality time in My glory will have enough fruit to feed nations!

"This is why I have told you in the past that I would only be using those who spend time daily with Us to advance My kingdom in this next revival. Only those who soak in My presence will be equipped to carry My glory to the nations. To represent Me as I truly am takes a life of intimate fellowship. I do have those who have paid that price, and I will be bringing them forth to use them to demonstrate My goodness and My love for all mankind.

"Many are called, but few are chosen. I have hand selected those who did hear My call and did respond with love to My invitation to get to know Me. These will be like this tree you see today in My garden. They will bear abundant fruit and will be used by Holy Spirit mightily. Many will be saved, delivered, healed and discipled by those few who love Me enough to die to themselves."

Looking about me, I saw many very tall, giant angels gathering the huge apples into enormous baskets. These angels had wings that weren't opened, but hung beside them. Jesus explained that they were bringing the fruit from this garden to God's children living in Heaven to enjoy; they would be eating fruit that was filled with His glory. His essence and presence filled these apples that grew in the glory.

My Father explained: "All Heaven is filled with My glory and all partake of it freely and fully. This can happen on the Earth, if more of My children will soak in My glory daily. The mammoth fruit they will produce will be filled with My glory, My essence and My presence, just like the fruit you see growing in My garden of glory in Heaven. This is why My Son taught you to pray that My will would be done on Earth as it is in Heaven.

"You just soak, spending quality time in My glory, and I will cause great fruit to be borne through your life. As you saw My mighty, majestic angels gather the fruit to feed the multitudes in Heaven, I will do the same on Earth. I will release these angels to gather your fruit and disburse it to the multitudes as you simply sit and soak. These trees in My garden of glory don't go forth and dispense their fruit. They are firmly rooted in My glory. You do the same; stay firmly planted in My presence and, with very little effort on your part, the fruit of a life lived in, for and through Me will be sent to My hungry children. My will shall be done on Earth as it is in Heaven, as you marinate in Us and believe in Our power to help you be fruitful."

> *...Therefore go and make disciples of all nations...* (Matthew 28:18–20).

Chapter Two

Growing in the Glory

But you are a shield around me, oh Lord; you bestow glory on me and lift up my head. To the Lord I cry aloud, and he answers me from his holy hill.

—Psalm 3:3–4

Sitting in my prayer room and quickly back in the spirit, I found myself sitting beside Jesus on the golden swing on the Mountain of Glory. Looking about me, I saw all the enormous, magnificent flowers surrounding us and heard Him say: "Do you see how My glory magnifies what is good? Do you see how soaking in My glory will make all that is good in you grow and multiply? Soaking in My glory is not just a preparation for ministry; it must become a lifestyle.

"Just like these plants, remain rooted in My glory and grow. If you stay firmly rooted in My glory, you will see miracles continually. Just say 'yes' to the invitation to abide in My glory, and Holy Spirit will help you live constantly in the glory. Sleep in the glory; eat in the glory, visit with others in the glory, talk on the phone in the glory, do your chores in the glory, and you will see miracles all the time. Miracles are the fruit of the glory! This is how I did all the miracles when I was on the Earth; I abided in My Father's glory constantly. That was how I could only do what I saw the Father do."

Listening to my Friend, I looked with eyes of faith and saw enormous plants whose leaves were as large as a table top. Then to my amazement, a very large elephant walked over to us. Jesus laughed at my startled reaction, and together we climbed on the back of the Lord's friendly pet. He accommodated us by kneeling on the ground and, once we were securely in place on his back, stood and began to take us for an enjoyable tour of this garden in glory.

Not only did I see magnificent, magenta flowers, yellow daffodils and plants and flowers galore, I saw animals you would expect to see in Africa. All of them were friendly, clean and very large. Macaws, parrots and all different sizes, kinds and colors of birds flew and landed on the garden's grandiose trees. Lions, giraffes, kangaroos and hyenas all mingled about us, as we rode along laughing and singing together. Yes, we sang love songs to one another in this garden that marinated in the glory of God.

All Are Invited to Soak in His Glory

Jesus said, "Many are invited to come to this place in the spirit in My kingdom, but few accept Our invitation to soak in Our glory. Once those few do come and bathe in Our glory, their spiritual eyes can be opened by faith, to see what you are observing today."

While riding on this very different mode of transportation, my Lord whispered in my ear, from the place behind me, where He sat holding me close to His chest: "For the few who take the time to sit apart with Us and just allow Us, by faith, to bring them into the glory realm, this is one of Our benefits. The longer and more frequently they immerse themselves in this tangible glory, the more the glory becomes part of them. My glory transforms and equips My children. A frightened Moses became a confident leader of a nation and a dear friend by soaking in My glory. My character merges with all who seek My face and settle for nothing less than My glory. We become one!"

Listening intently, and basking in the love His words held, I was interrupted by the gentle elephant, as he swung his trunk from in front of him to me. His trunk held a beautiful, fragrant bouquet of flowers, which he dropped into my arms. Such joy filled my heart, because I knew these flowers were a gift from Jesus, who laughed heartily at my delight. I leaned forward and patted the head of my Lord's pet elephant and couldn't help myself from hugging him, as I held my flowers close to my heart.

To be loved like this was what my heart needed and my Jesus knew it. Many times on the Earth I found myself neglected, misunderstood, judged and cast aside, but not here! Today my heart felt cherished, loved, honored and accepted. My Jesus knows how to heal the wounds of a broken heart! If we let Him, by drawing close, leaving our trials and hurts behind, and just immersing ourselves in His embrace, He will heal every wound.

The Benefits of His Glory Revealed

"I am showing you today the benefits of My glory. It is not just a wonderful loving feeling that overwhelms you. It is much more than that. It makes giants out of the seemingly insignificant ones. It creates an atmosphere where faith is ignited so that miracles can occur. Like corn kernels, when heat is applied to them, take on an entirely different manifestation and identity as popcorn, so too My glory transforms the identities of those who bask in it.

"Soaking in My love—My presence—this is where the power and gift of miracles comes from. In the river of compassion, My love flows and healing happens; never will religion bear the fruit of miracles. That deep, holy, abiding, devoted, loving relationship always produces miracles and answered prayers. There is no shortcut to receiving the gift of miracles. In order for your shadow to heal the sick and deliver the oppressed, you must soak in My love daily. As I went before My Father daily to get the love, power, wisdom and strength I needed for My ministry, you do the same. If you do this, you, too, will operate in the same power I did. Yes, I promised that greater things you would do than I did, as you do what I did: live devoted to My Father."

> *I tell you the truth, anyone who has faith in me will do what I have been doing. He will do even greater things than these, because I am going to the Father* (John 14:12).

The Glory Seekers' Rewards

"Yes, I created all the animals for My children to enjoy, but I also created them for My enjoyment, too," my Friend explained, as I wondered why there were so many animals that walked throughout this garden on Heaven's golden mountain.

Then to my great delight, we came upon a family of lions—mom and dad, with their cubs, all relaxing in the sun with flowers and shrubs all around them. My Lord's elephant knelt down, and Jesus and I climbed off. Hand in hand, we walked over to the friendly lions. Sitting down amongst them, Jesus picked up a little lion cub. He hugged it and held it high, laughing the whole time, and then handed it to me. Oh, what joy filled my heart, as this little one cuddled in my arms! What delight was ours, beyond what words could describe!

During my visit here, I wondered why this gold Mountain of Glory was so special. I knew that all Heaven was filled with God's glory. While playing with the lion cubs, Jesus, always knowing my thoughts, explained why this garden on Heaven's Mountain of Glory was unique:

"This is a place Father has made for those few who bathe in His glory while on the Earth. Only those who spend time in His glory while living on the Earth are allowed entry, once they come to Heaven to live forever. This garden is one of their rewards. Because they have spent long hours in the glory, when they come to dwell in Heaven and visit this garden, the animals who live here recognize them and greet them, as they enter through the golden, white picket fence. Many are the rewards of the faithful and this is one reserved for those who live in and long for Our glory."

Chapter Three

Meeting His Children in the Garden of Glory

Then little children were brought to Jesus for him to place his hands on them and pray for them.

—Matthew 19:13

Weeks later, while sitting between Father and Jesus on the golden swing that was lined with beautiful, shimmering gold, brocade cushions, overshadowed by Holy Spirit, my spiritual eyes were opened wide to see wonders that flooded my soul with delight.

Sweet, gentle kittens sat on our laps, crawled upon our chest and even nestled on our shoulders. Basking in the love of my Father, Jesus, Holy Spirit and Their pets, to my amazement, I beheld a very tall, handsome giraffe standing right in front of us. This giraffe bent his long neck down and gave me a kiss. The love of my Father just flooded my soul, as I calmly received His affection through this giraffe.

Looking to my left, beside the swing lay another friend of my God. A magnificent male lion with his family, just basking in the love of my Father. So quiet was this family of lions that I would not have seen them if Father and Jesus hadn't coaxed me to look beside the swing. Then I felt our swing start to move forward toward the lanky giraffe. Looking behind us, expecting to see one of Father's angels pushing His swing, I saw a very large, dark brown gorilla. This gorilla was a happy fellow; it was evident that he felt proud that he was allowed the privilege of pushing Father and Jesus, as they laughed heartily and were thoroughly enjoying the ride.

Father spoke: "Do you see the wonders I have prepared for My faithful sons and daughters? Enjoy today what someday you will be allowed to partake of continually. Love abounds in My glory. Once My glory is showered upon all, no one will be able to escape My great love.

"What I show you, few have seen; that is why We ask you to write and to speak about these wonders. We want Our children to know about some of the rewards they will receive when they come home to live with Us forever. It will bring great comfort to those who grieve over their loved ones who have left them, and now dwell here in Our kingdom. It will also inspire many to remain faithful—no matter what—both in the good times and in the trials. Yes, hearing these revelations will help My children to be heavenly minded and to think on those things that are good and pure and lovely. That way they can be refocused on Me rather than absorbed with the things they are enduring. Hearing these revelations will also help their minds to more easily ascend in the spirit where We dwell. Delight will replace dread when they hear what We want them to know.

"There will be those who will discount what you say. Ignore their critical remarks, because there will be many who know for certain that what you have seen and heard is true. Some will have had dreams of what you have seen in the spirit, and they will rejoice knowing I have spoken to them, too."

Sitting back and relaxing in this heavenly encounter, I saw the enormous, flowering apple tree; colorful parrots, macaws and other elegant birds fly about, going from limb to limb. The rainbow sky, the fragrant flowers and the loving creatures made my heart soar with joy, but what filled my heart the most was the love and glory pouring off Father, Jesus and Holy Spirit.

As my visit ended, Father said, "More and more of My children will be seeing wonders from Heaven, because this is the hour when those things that have been hidden will be exposed."

An Astounding Revelation in the Garden of Glory

Weeks later, while sitting quietly in prayer for a few hours, not seeing or hearing anything, suddenly I felt the love of God pour over me. His great glory took my breath away and brought tears of joy to my eyes. In an instant, I was back in the spirit in His garden of glory. The brightest, biggest, boldest flowers appeared before my spiritual eyes. My heart soared with such pleasure; it was hard to contain the joy I felt.

Then, out of nowhere, a very large, brightly colored beach ball came bouncing down the flower laden path right into my arms. I knew this was a very special invitation I was receiving. With my heavenly Tour Guide beside me, I ran like a teenager down the path to a beach.

The beach was like no other I had ever seen on Earth, or on other visits to Heaven. The water was not rough, but waves appeared, to the delight of the children waiting to ride them on their boogie boards and colorful flotation devices. Children—gleeful, happy, excited children—were all over this very large ocean beach. Some children were playing together in the water, but many others were playing in the sand, making all different creatures, castles, and vehicles out of the sand that lined the shore.

When I looked closely, with my eyes of faith opened wide, I saw that the beach sand was made of coarse gold dust. One child even made a big beetle out of this gold and then jumped on it. He lay in the mound of the golden sand, laughing with his arms and legs moving, so as to make sure he completely smashed his creation. Then covered in golden sand, he ran to the shore and jumped in the inviting, refreshing water. Some children made elaborate castles and played with their friends about them. All over this glowing beach were many of the artistic creations the Father's children had spent long hours making. No one wrecked anyone's work of art; respect for each other filled this loving, joy filled atmosphere.

While enjoying a swim with the children and Jesus, my Lord instructed me: "Let the children both here and on Earth come to you. Let them close to you, for we have given you a gift for children of all ages; let them close, so Our love in you can pour out on them and Our love in them can pour out on you."

With Jesus beside me, the children and I played, riding the waves, sliding down the large waterslides and diving off the rafts that floated in this delightful ocean of love. Yes, love was pouring forth from the waters—the love of Father that pours out of everything in Heaven—washed over all of us. Sounds of giggles, hearty laughter, squeals of delight and shouts of, "Look at me!" were heard.

The Father's Justice Revealed

In the midst of this beautiful time in Heaven, curiosity and wonder filled my mind, and I asked Jesus why these children were here in the garden of glory. In the past, I saw children in Heaven playing games, swimming, climbing trees and picnicking. I wondered why these children were at this very special beach in Heaven. Jesus answered my questions, as He always does, with deep satisfaction in His voice.

I knew He was waiting for me to ask Him this question, so He could tell me a wonderful truth: "These children are the offspring of the glory seekers on the Earth. Their parents lost them, either in the womb or during their childhood. Death took them from them. They are here enjoying the rich rewards their parents earned by seeking My glory."

Wow, I thought, "How blessed these children were to have parents that sought after God." What joy was theirs; to be able to visit this garden of glory, knowing that the devotion their parents poured out on God had purchased them a free ticket to this magnificent beach! Understanding the deep love their parents had for Father was one of the reasons their delight was so immense.

Jesus explained, "Daughter, I am a rewarder of those who diligently seek Me. Today I am showing you My justice. On the Earth, children inherit what their parents leave them when they die. These children were taken before their parents, so they lost their earthly inheritance. I am making sure they gain their heavenly inheritance that they will also someday enjoy with their parents when they join them in My kingdom.

"Encourage My children to diligently seek My glory, My will, and My presence because My rewards are astounding!"

> *His mercy extends to those who fear him, from generation to generation.... He has helped his servant Israel, remembering to be merciful to Abraham and his descendants forever, even as he said to our fathers* (Luke 1:50, 54).

Father and Jesus Interacting with Heaven's Children

After a few hours of sitting in my prayer room and waiting for my Lord and my Father's presence, suddenly I was deep in the spirit sitting in the garden of glory on the gold embossed, cushioned swing between Father and Jesus. While watching the scene unfold before me, I felt the outpouring of Father and Jesus' glory and love flow within and outside me. I was being saturated in love, so much so, that it brought tears of devotion and deep appreciation to my eyes.

I saw the magnificent apple tree in full bloom, covered in pink flowers in front of us, the rainbow sky high above, the gleeful, brightly colored birds flying about and Father's and Jesus's pets all around us. Then I heard the sound of children laughing and talking, and I even heard loud, childlike squeals of delight. A teenage boy was leading this group of little ones; it was evident that he took his responsibility of leading his charges quite seriously. He was guiding them from the beach to this heavenly garden, to visit Father and Jesus.

Like Holy Spirit guides us on the Earth to come for a visit with our God, this boy was doing the same. All were excited and eagerly followed his instructions to wait their turn to jump on Father's and Jesus' laps. Even though some of these little ones were soaking wet from their swim in the ocean of love, they were still welcome to sit on Their laps. Lots of hugs and kisses, secrets whispered in ears, giggles and hearty laughter are what I observed from my seat between my Friends. Twin little girls, dressed in identical, frilly, pink dresses, laughed, holding hands, while waiting their turn, where among the many, sweet children I saw. I was watching the scripture being fulfilled before my spiritual eyes:

> *Let the little children come to me, and do not hinder them, for the kingdom of heaven belongs to such as these* (Matthew 19:1).

These children were accompanied by their pets. Some children held fluffy kittens, others adorable puppies, and full-grown dogs walked beside many. The young fellow who was in charge wore a baseball cap. He was dressed like a typical teenager in shorts, a T-shirt that was embossed with diamonds and really cool sunglasses. It was evident that his pet monkey, who sat on his shoulder, felt honored to be his companion.

Love Abounds

While watching this loving scene take place before me, I thought of the time years ago when Jesus brought me to Hell. Each time I went there to observe what was going on, I saw the souls trapped in this place of great torment, mistreating one another. Prodded on by the demons ruling over them, they readily inflicted pain on their fellow sufferers.

Not so in Heaven. Love abounded here! Everyone helped one another. Not even one child pushed another boy or girl out of the way so they could get closer to Father and Jesus. In fact, they eagerly helped their buddies to climb on the Father and Jesus' laps. No one rushed another so they could have their turn; they patiently stood and enjoyed watching their friends absorb all the love that was being poured out on them. So much love poured out over the children, and it was hard for me to tell who was enjoying themselves more—the children or Father and Jesus.

Scattered amongst this large, happy group of children were angels dressed in shimmering white garments and holding babies in their arms. Waiting, and watching these special children soak up the love of Father and Jesus, they brought their little charges to be held, hugged and kissed by God the Father and His Son Jesus.

Nestling in even closer to Father and Jesus, Father told me: "I am never too busy to love My children here in Heaven and on the Earth. As you do visit us and receive our love daily, all are invited to do the same. I made you for that purpose, so you could receive My love and return your affection to Us. Yes, this garden of glory is reserved as a very special treat for the glory seekers and their offspring, but all are welcome to join the ranks of the glory seekers by just seeking My presence and getting apart with Us. What you see here is duplicated daily in My kingdom—all are welcome. You were made for love and nothing else truly satisfies My children—only love. My love pouring forth on all who will gather before Me. Love abounds in My kingdom, and hatred—only hatred—abounds in satan's domain."

Chapter Four

LESSONS LEARNED ON THE MOUNTAIN OF GLORY

You are those who stood by me in my trials. And I confer on you a kingdom, just as my Father conferred one on me, so that you may eat and drink at my table in my kingdom and sit on thrones, judging the twelve tribes of Israel.

—LUKE 27:28–30

One sunny morning while waiting for my Lord to visit me, I saw Jesus. He appeared in a vision to me on His majestic, white horse and invited me to ride behind Him. Immediately, I climbed on behind Jesus, on His horse's very comfortable seat. Off we galloped in the spirit, to a place on the Mountain of Glory I had not been to before. Up the steep, golden mountain we rode, so smoothly it felt like we were riding on a cloud. Past the garden of glory we went, and with great speed, we kept climbing higher.

Jesus Brings me to See His Angel Armies

Then to my amazement, I saw angels of all sizes lining this golden pathway. The Commander in Chief of Heaven's armies, dressed all in white, riding on His stately, white horse was taking me in the spirit, dressed in white and seated behind Him, to command His angels to do His bidding. As I pressed my face into my Lord's shoulders, I knew what I was supposed to do.

While passing by each group of angels, I looked closely and saw that some were very tall with bronze-like skin, others were medium height and were dressed in garments with gold belts and loose pants. They looked like soldiers ready for battle, with long swords held beside them. Some were extremely tall and dressed in flowing, white, rainbow, translucent garments with large, white feathered wings. These angels had gold bands around their foreheads. It appeared that they were assembled in their ranks awaiting orders from their Commander in Chief.

As Jesus and I rode by each contingent of angels, Jesus prompted me to send the angels forth to Earth to do His bidding. I began telling the angels of truth to: "Go bring truth wherever there are lies being told and believed. Bring freedom to those held captive in addictions and by all evil. Bring fire and love for Father and Jesus to the lukewarm. Bring hope to the hopeless. Bring body parts from the body parts room in Heaven to those who need new kidneys, new hearts, new brains." I continued commanding Jesus' angel armies to go to Earth and bring God's will forth—that His will would be done on Earth as it is in Heaven.

My Friend explained, "Today I am showing you how to partner with My heavenly hosts. Stay pure (the white garments), cleave to Me by staying in intimate fellowship with Me (hugging Jesus), then be led by My Spirit, as Holy Spirit shows you what We want done. In answer to the prayers of Our children, send My angels forth to do My bidding. Yes, We have given you governmental authority—a governmental anointing—to use in this hour in prayer. Daily I will bring you with Me in the spirit, to activate and to release My angels to perform My will on the Earth."

Authority to Command Angels

The following day, I was once again in the spirit, and saw myself riding behind Jesus on His white horse. He took me much higher onto the Mountain of Glory, than where I had been the day before. Assembled below us were Heavens' angel armies. For as far as I could see, there were multitudes of angels waiting for their orders.

I asked my Lord, why were the angels assembled on the Mountain of Glory, instead of any other place in Heaven. He explained:

"Demons cannot stand My glory; they are undone and lose all strength in the glory. My glory is a mighty weapon that disarms demons and empowers My children. My angels absorb My glory and release it when they appear on the Earth. This is why so many of My children, when they encounter My messengers, are undone and fall on their faces in their presence. It is my children experiencing My glory pouring off the angels. My angels bring My glory to the Earth and do release it wherever they are sent. They do overcome evil with an abundance of good! Fire from Heaven falls and purges My little ones of evil.

"Send my angels forth!" He declared. "Because we are one, daughter, you can speak My words, and My messengers will perform those words. Only those who abide in Us, know Us well and truly live for Us, can command angels, because it is Holy Spirit commanding them through you. All others who say they are Ours, but are not, waste their time, because they have no true authority and cannot influence the spirit realm, neither angelic nor demonic! Only those who are connected to the vine can bear fruit! I say, always stay connected to Us, with your time spent in Our courts, and your desires one with Ours! Encourage My children to develop close, continual fellowship with Us and they, too, will command angels and demons and be very fruitful."

Exchanging Bricks for Feathers

To my great delight, the Lord appeared to me in my prayer room one sunny morning. He was dressed in humble attire; He had a garment on that seemed to be off-white cotton, and on His feet, I saw brown sandals. He was laughing and kept coaxing me to come away with Him into the spirit. I fell at His feet, in the spirit, and put my head in His lap. Instinctively, I brought to Him all the people I have been praying for. As I told Him each thing I was concerned about, He reassured me that He would take care of everything.

Quite a while later, after finishing my long list of requests, He laughed and said, "Now are you ready to come with Me? I want you to leave all your cares in My hands, and let's go see what I want to show you today." As He spoke, I could see His long, dark brown hair falling on the sides of His face and His handsome smile, while He looked so kindly at me.

Leaving all my cares behind, I got up, put my hand in His and walked into the spirit with my compassionate Friend. Encouraging me, He said: "I understand how overwhelmed you feel when you see My children suffer as they do, at the hands of sinful man and afflicted by the enemy with sickness, disease and strongholds of wickedness. It breaks My heart, too, My friend. I want you to take a break from all this and come apart with Me."

Instantly, we were far away in the spirit walking through one of Heaven's flower gardens. "Don't rush through this garden, but take a minute to pick a flower, enjoy the fragrance and listen to the melody My flowers are singing to Me. Come on, let's just rest in this garden of love, My friend," Jesus said, as He invited me to stop and lay down amongst these beautiful flowers.

There was no darkness here, but the light of His glory just flooded me completely. "This is what My children need. Just as you find yourself overwhelmed by the concerns of life, so do most of My people. Teach them how to give Me all that bothers them, and then tell them to enter the spirit with Us, where they can encounter Our glory."

> *Come to me, all you who are weary and burdened, and I will give you rest… For my yoke is easy and my burden is light* (Matthew 11:28–30).

As He spoke, I remembered what He revealed to me a few days earlier when we were sitting together. During that encounter, Jesus showed me that everything I was concerned about was like heavy bricks piled up in front of me. As He stood before me, I gave these issues, or heavy bricks, to Jesus, and they suddenly turned into light feathers. Where I had seen problems and difficulties, now I saw feathers falling about me. I realized if I continued staying focused on my problems, or if I kept carrying these bricks wherever I went, it would hinder me from entering the spirit, where I could get apart with Him.

Gathering my thoughts, and filled with His peace and His great love, I looked about me to discover what Heaven's garden held for me to see today. Brilliant, colorful butterflies flew about us. I was able to easily touch and hold these gentle, calm, soft visitors. Looking to my right side, I saw little fluffy, light brown rabbits playing amongst the flowers. Then Jesus said softly in my left ear, "See what you would have missed today, if you didn't leave your concerns with Me and come apart in the spirit."

Serving in Heaven

Hearing a noise, I sat up and looked behind us, and to my delight, there stood Father's friendly, tall giraffe. Now I knew we were in the garden of glory that I had visited weeks ago. Walking with Jesus through the flower bed, to visit His friendly giraffe, I saw a baby giraffe scampering behind its mother. Jesus handed me a large baby bottle filled with warm milk to feed this young one. Revelation came tumbling upon me, and I knew why Jesus came to see me in His casual clothes. Today we were visiting His pets to act as servants, or caretakers, for them. Even in Heaven we are encouraged to serve one another.

Jesus explained, "Yes, daughter, in My kingdom, angels are not the only ones who serve others, but all show their love by serving one another. The greatest of all is the servant of all! Serving one another, here in Heaven and on Earth, brings joy and helps My people to forget about themselves and to think of others. To selfishly look for others to cater to your needs only brings sorrow and fuels disappointment. Imagine if everyone sought to serve others, what joy would be present! This is what Heaven is like—a place where love, joy, selflessness and service to others abound. The more My children seek to serve others while living on Earth, the more they will encounter some of the atmosphere of Heaven."

Pondering this visitation, I realized that the Lord came to me dressed in His lowly garment, as a servant. He knew I was burdened by many cares, and He had come to serve me. Jesus took me, in the spirit to the Garden of Glory, to restore my peace and joy, to refresh and to strengthen me. In this encounter, His creatures poured love and affection on me and at the same time, His presence inspired me. Then to my wonder, He taught me a valuable lesson; serving is one of the keys to finding happiness. Serving is so essential to living a joyful life, everyone in Heaven serves one another—even Jesus!

> *If anyone wants to be first, he must be the very last, and the servant of all* (Mark 9:33-37).

Once I was renewed by Heaven's service to me, I was able to begin serving again—feeding the baby giraffe its bottle. This is why it is so important to serve others. Many have grown weary serving, and need a helping hand to encourage them, so they can get back up and continue to serve those in need of help.

Jesus also showed me that we are not alone in serving others. He handed me the baby bottle. I did not have to go and find it, fill it with milk and warm it up. Jesus just gave it to me. In the same way, He will give us whatever we need, to help us serve others.

> *Whoever wants to become great among you must be your servant* (Matthew 20:20-28).

Chapter Five

Jesus Brings Me to See a Stable in Heaven

The Lord thunders at the head of his army;
his forces are beyond number....
—Joel 2:11

Alone in my prayer room, sitting in the Lord's presence, this sunny day I felt led to pray in my prayer language. The longer I prayed in tongues, the greater I experienced the anointing and even His glory. Then, suddenly a staircase appeared before me in the spirit. Jesus stood at the base of this golden stairway and invited me to climb into Heaven with Him. Immediately, I ran to Him and gleefully climbed far away from my cozy prayer room, into the spirit realm.

"Today I am going to take you to a stable in Heaven," He explained, as we climbed through the clouds above, into the soft blue sky. It felt like only seconds past, and we were walking into a large, red stable. Stalls lined either side of the long passageway. The Lord led me from stall to stall, where I saw the most fantastic horses imaginable: one was all white, another shiny black with white hooves, another was a palomino with a light tan, long mane and tail, another was chestnut brown in color. Each one was beautiful, and all were warm, loving and welcoming. The Lord handed me a shiny, large red apple and said, "Here, feed them these apples. They love apples!" Together we went from one stall to another, feeding these gentle giants their delicious treats. Angels helped us by unbolting each stall; it was apparent they were the caretakers of the Lord's treasured horses.

"Come, let us go for a ride," my Friend said as His angels led two of the horses out of their stalls, put soft comfortable saddles on them and helped me mount my shiny, black stallion. Jesus, laughing with approval at my delight, sat watching from His magnificent, white horse. I knew His horse was very special to Him and so did the horse and the angels. Horse and rider loved each other, and thoroughly enjoyed one another's company.

"We are going on a picnic," my Lord declared, interrupting my thoughts. I looked about but saw no picnic basket, and my Friend explained, "Oh, My angels have gone before us and have prepared our lunch for us."

Off we rode beside each other, just laughing and talking about the glories of Heaven: the rolling green pastures, the rainbow sky above us, and the fragrant flower beds that line the riding paths. I was enjoying myself so much; I wished I would never have to leave. Instantly my Lord said, "Daughter, you know someday you will come and live here forever, but you still have much to do on the Earth before that day comes." I laughed, knowing He always has a wonderful plan and my best interest in mind.

After a wonderful, relaxing ride, we came upon the Lord's picnic grove. Jesus helped me get off my friendly horse and led me to the picnic lunch that His angels so lovingly prepared for us. Sitting down on the soft, red and white checkered blanket, we begin eating all the delicious food. "When you come to live here, My friend, you will have your own horse and your own stable, just like the one I brought you to today. It will be full of loving, strong, devoted horses for you to enjoy and share with your friends."

I asked my Lord, "Does everyone get their own horses when they come to Heaven?"

He explained, "No, only those who have earned this reward will get this eternal blessing. That is why We are giving you a stable filled with horses, so that when your friends visit, they can go horseback riding with you. In the same way, not everyone will earn the reward of an indoor pool in their mansion, but they can come and swim with you in yours.

"Daughter, encourage My children to live their lives fully for Us, so that they can receive all the wonderful treasures We have prepared for them in Heaven. The more they love Us, spend time with Us, share Our love with others and live in obedience to Us, the more rewards We can pour out on them."

As we talked and ate, I watched our two horses graze. They were having a picnic, too, and they were enjoying listening to the voice of their Master, as He spoke tenderly to me. "Lord," I asked, "will one of these horses be mine when I come to live in Heaven?"

Laughing, Jesus explained, "When you come home, I will lead you to My stable, and you will be allowed to choose your very own horses. Each one will be different, but each one will be filled with the love that abides in all in Heaven."

Then I saw the staircase peering through the ground and knew it was time to leave. I also realized that if I stayed much longer, it would have been terribly difficult to leave. My Lord accompanied me down the staircase and back to my prayer room where His glory filled my heart and flooded me with the joy I felt in Heaven. Sitting in my chair, I kept repeating, "Someday I will have my own horse—my own horses to love and to ride—someday!"

HIS GLORY REVEALED IN TIMES OF INTIMACY

And we, who with unveiled faces all reflect the Lord's glory, are being transformed into his likeness with ever increasing glory, which comes from the Lord who is the Spirit.

—2 Corinthians 3:18

Chapter Six

THE WAY OF TEMPTATIONS AND TRICKS

The arrogant dig pitfalls for me, contrary to your law.

—PSALM 119: 85

Suddenly, as out of nowhere, I heard wonderful Father say, "I am a God who takes great pleasure in loving those who seek Me; who truly seek to know Me. As a diamond has many facets, there are many facets of who I am. Daily let Me show you a new facet of My being."

He continued, "Trust Me to reveal, by My Spirit, who I am to you, so you in turn can reveal My Son to the nations. Whoever sees Me, sees My Son. We are one; be one with Us. Revelation birthed by My Spirit brings freedom. Set the captives free with words birthed from My heart to yours!"

Such excitement filled my being when I heard my Father invite me on a closer walk with Him; I realized that the God who created the universe and sustains it invited me to know Him, to hear His thoughts and understand His ways better. His heart was calling out to mine. He wanted to unveil Himself before me daily, so

I would know Him well, know what He thinks about the issues we face in life and love Him more; because to know Him and to understand His ways is to love Him.

In this section of *The Glory of God Revealed* I will share some of the encounters I had with Father, Jesus and Holy Spirit that will help you to know our God better. Then you, too, will love Him more, as you understand many new facets of who He is, as well as what He thinks and feels about the many issues we face in our lives!

Overcoming Obstacles to Get to Him

Absorbed in His presence and filled with His overwhelming love, I entered a realm in the spirit where divine revelations and astonishing truths were about to cascade upon my life. I came to a passageway in the spirit that was blocked by large boulders. Climbing them appeared impossible. But I knew my King was on the other side. Suddenly, I saw a small mouse scamper by and crawl through a space at the bottom of this wall of boulders. I removed some small rocks around this tiny hole and was able to squeeze through to the other side.

When I stood to my feet, I was totally amazed at what I saw. A palatial room stood before me. Gold walls with beautiful, brocade burgundy drapes, delightfully elaborate furnishings and magnificent paintings dazzled my incredulous eyes. My King sat on His golden throne across the room and beckoned me to come and sit with Him. I ran over, delighted that I had found Him, and to think, a little mouse led me to my Friend. I was reminded again that His ways are not our ways. Dynamite didn't remove the wall, nor did a heavy bulldozer, but a small mouse showed me the way into His presence. Giving up and turning back was an option, but the mouse scampered by me through the tiny passageway, before I seriously considered giving up the pursuit of His presence.

Sitting beside Him He welcomed me: "I've been waiting for you My friend. What took you so long? I have made the way for you, but many times you have allowed the boulders of memories and concerns block your way into My presence. Distractions can make the way impassable, but as you turn to Me, I will show you the way where I dwell waiting to fill you with My peace. Come; let's go for a walk."

Following Jesus into the Realm of Revelation

The Lord rose to His feet, took my hand in His and together we left the elaborate room, through the tall, curtained lined doorway. A great darkness enveloped us as we entered this new area. Instantly I became afraid.

Encouraging me, He said: "Don't be afraid, My friend. Remember I am the light of the world. Wherever you go, My light shines upon you. Don't fear the darkness or the unknown, because I know all things, and I lead you in the way you are to go."

To my surprise, we were back in the long passageway that led to Hell that I had visited years before with Jesus. This dingy, dark hall was covered with cobwebs. Encouraging me to come with Him, My Lord explained: "Don't shrink back, My friend. I know you would rather Me bring you into the glorious place where I dwell in My kingdom, but today it is necessary that I take you to where My children are suffering at the hands of My enemy."

Holding tightly to His hand, I continued walking forward, trying to keep my eyes fixed on Him, as He taught me in the past. It was imperative that I look at this place through Him, or it would be unbearable. Cobwebs of hatred hung everywhere. Cold and damp, this corridor had slime running down its walls. Spiders ran through the slime and wove it into the intricate webs. Unlike any other cobwebs I had seen, they glistened from the slime that coated many of the fibers in the webs.

Jesus warned: "Stay close, daughter. Don't let the sparkle on the webs lure you away from Me. It is still a deadly trap, even though it looks inviting because of its shimmering, delicate design. The enemy is not stupid. He makes his traps enticing. Remember, he is a master of deception. He can make evil look good and even inviting."

From a distance, these webs looked like they had diamonds scattered beautifully all throughout their intricate design. I had to remind myself that they were made of slime. Fearing that these webs would touch me and impart their deadly venom into me, I clung closer to Jesus. The more I focused on Jesus and the closer I got to Him, the clearer I could see and the greater I could understand the terrible traps these webs would become.

Jesus interjected: "Yes, daughter, just touching the slime does impart the subtle venom of evil into you. It is designed to entice you into a sinful lifestyle and draw you into the place where there is no way of escape. You are right to avoid the glistening slime of the enemy at all costs. As My people walk through life, so many things appear good to them, but they are not. Rather, they are the device of the enemy to draw them off the right path into the pit he has set before them."

Jesus stopped walking. Directly in front of us loomed a deep, dark pit. If I hadn't been so close to Jesus, I would have fallen into it. The webs with their distracting shimmer and the dense darkness made me completely unaware of this chasm.

The Subtle Deception Lurking on the Passageway of Life

"Things are not always as they appear," Jesus cautioned. "You must stay close to Me, so that I can expose every pitfall. This place is not Hell, but one of the corridors that leads so many there. Tricks and temptations line the walls of this passageway through life. As you walk along this passage, there are many pitfalls, but fear not. I will lead all who are close to Me, past the pits, and keep them from being allured by the slime of the enemy, into the web of deception he has spun for them."

When I looked at the webs again, they no longer looked beautiful and inviting like lacey diamonds. Now I saw them as they truly were—grotesquely ugly. Smokey black webs, with no pattern to them, and putrid, green slime hanging all over the webs disgusted me. How could they have appeared as beautiful a few minutes ago? I never saw anything so ugly and repulsive.

My Teacher explained: "This is how the enemy fools My children. He makes evil look beautiful and inviting. Once My children take hold of the web that has been spun for them, and they are ensnared by it, with no way of escape, the enemy reveals the truth of what has captured them. It gives him great pleasure to see the anguish of those who hate and are repulsed by those things that formerly held a great attraction to them.

"All their hatred and revulsion of these evil things that hold them captive cannot set them free. As they struggle with this hatred and try to escape, it only causes them to be more ensnared by its web. Daughter, there is no escape from such bondage apart from Me. Just as I protected you as you walked through this corridor of temptation, anyone who calls out to Me will receive the same protection and care. Those that have been deceived and ensnared will be plucked free by Me as they sincerely cry out to Me for help. I am the way of escape for all who truly turn to Me.

"All that have fallen into these pits along this pathway can be saved as well. Walking around the bottom of the pit, trying to climb out by themselves, standing on others to try to get out, or just kicking and hating the pit are all vain efforts and of no avail. These attempts to get free only cause the pit to be made deeper. Anyone and everyone who calls out to Me will be lifted out and put back on the solid path that leads to life and joy."

While listening to the Lord, I observed large, black eagles fly over the web-entrenched, pit-strewn corridor and grab lifeless victims with their sharp talons and roughly pull them out of the pits. They had lost their lives struggling in the web that completely wrapped around them. The eagles easily plucked them out of the web that had stolen their lives and flew off with them.

In the distance, I could see dense smoke arising out of a massive, flaming chasm. When the eagles approached the furnace-like cavern, loud cheers emanated from the demons guarding it, as they dropped their victims into the flaming hole.

Watching this horrifying scene, I grabbed more tightly to Jesus and cried out, "Jesus save me, help me!"

Without Him, I knew I was no different from those who had been ensnared and deceived. He was my only hope of escape.

Jesus explained, "What I am showing you is the truth. You have seen one of the paths of life through My eyes today, daughter. Many fall prey to the enemy on this path, the Way of Temptations and Tricks. Don't play with temptations or toy with the tricks of the enemy, and you will stay secure on the path of life."

Walking the Path of Life with Jesus

Instantly, while the Lord spoke these words, we rose out of this dark, ugly corridor to the path Jesus and I so often walked on together. It was grassy, steep and had rocks strewn about it, but it was sunny and alive with life. Birds chirped, butterflies flittered by, and the fragrance of the flowers that dotted the landscape filled the air. In the distance, I could hear the ocean waves crashing on the shore. This place was not perfect like the garden in Heaven I had previously visited, but it was peaceful and teeming with life.

Jesus coaxed, "Come, follow Me upon the path that leads to My kingdom. Those that look for an easy way to find eternal happiness quickly fall upon the corridor of Temptations and Tricks. The way I will lead you is not always comfortable or easy. Some days the way is steep and tiring, other days your feet may stumble on the rocks that are strewn about the path, and often clouds may appear and the rains will come, but this is the only way to come into the glories of My kingdom.

"Keep close to Me," He said, "and I will be the light in every storm cloud and the shelter from the rains of disappointment. Though the path may be strewn with rocks and even boulders at times, I will help you surmount every obstacle. My abiding joy will fill you, just like the fragrance from the flowers fills the air. Though the way is steep at times, there will be seasons of rest along the way. If you keep your hand in Mine, and your eyes fixed on Me, I promise you will make it to the top."

This was just one of the paths the Lord would bring me to in the following days. Because of His great love and faithfulness toward His children, like a dutiful parent, He revealed many truths to me, reminded me of lessons I'd forgotten, and warned me of hazards we will surely meet on the path of life. His desire is that we follow His ways on the Earth, so that we can join Him someday in His glorious kingdom in Heaven and enjoy all the glories that He has prepared for those who love Him.

> *Forgetting what is behind and straining toward what is ahead, I press on toward the goal to win the prize for which God has called me heavenward in Christ Jesus* (Philippians 3:13-14).

Chapter Seven

Taking Time to Swim in the River of Love

Swarms of living creatures will live wherever the river flows...Fruit trees of all kinds will grow on both banks of the river. Their leaves will not wither, nor will their fruit fail. Every month they will bear, because the water from the sanctuary flows to them. Their fruit will serve for food and their leaves for healing.

—Ezekiel 47:9,12

Early one morning, the Lord invited me to go for a swim in the spirit realm. As soon as I responded affirmatively, a warm and inviting river appeared directly in front of me. Without stopping, I walked with my Friend into the water. A tremendous feeling of overwhelming love enveloped me, as my feet splashed in the water. Launching out into the deep waters, my Lord beckoned me to go under water with Him. To my amazement, I could breathe and see clearly, while I swam in this special spiritual river of love and glory.

Softly Jesus said: "I invite all My friends to come into this river with Me, but many do not follow Me here. It takes time to come to this place of sweet fellowship; most of My people are too busy to spend their time with Me.

"It is vital for the health and well-being of My friends for them to enter this place of relaxation and healing. As one enters My river, all the wounds that naturally come from interacting with others are healed. The wounds of rejection, jealousy, contempt and ridicule are washed away with great ease. I am God; all things are possible, even easy, for Me.

"Peace and love dance upon this supernatural water and infiltrate all who immerse themselves here. Blinders are removed from the eyes of those who have been taught to see things incorrectly. Vision and truth are imparted and replace every lie. Ears that are deaf to the heartbreaking cries of My children are suddenly opened. Wisdom, one of My greatest gifts, instantly fills minds, as understanding imparts her truths through the waters of My presence.

"Immerse yourself in My river of glory frequently, and spiritual dryness, the spirit of religion, won't be able to touch you. All things are made new in My river. The old and the stale are replaced by the fresh and the vibrant. New mindsets are embraced in My river and fresh revelation imparted."

He ended our visit with this word of wisdom: "Come and swim in My river, My presence, daily, for the health of your soul is at stake. Let nothing so preoccupy you, not even serving Me or My children, that you forfeit the time spent with Me in My river."

He Is a Wall of Fire Protecting Us

> *And Daniel could understand visions and dreams of all kinds* (Daniel 1:17).

In a dream one night, the Lord taught me another benefit His presence affords us, during the storms the enemy so frequently sends our way. In this very vivid dream, a lion had been spotted in the area where a group of us lived. We decided to take turns keeping guard, so that the lion wouldn't sneak in and attack us while we were sleeping. When we woke up, we discovered that one of the guards had been dragged off during the night by the vicious lion. All the precautions we used didn't help us against this sneaky, cruel predator.

I brought the dream to Jesus for Him to explain the meaning to me:

"The Word reminds you to be on guard, because your enemy prowls around like a vicious lion seeking whomever he will devour. As you saw in the dream, all the precautions taken didn't protect you from this brutal beast. Apart from Me, there is no protection from the enemy. I am a wall of fire protecting you. My blood provides a shield that nothing evil can penetrate. All your efforts to keep the enemy from you and yours are fruitless. A city, without a wall of protection surrounding it and a locked gate at its entrance, is an open target for enemy forces.

"Walk with Me in My presence, and you will be like a walled city, safe and secure continually, that no enemy can penetrate. Walking in My presence is the only way to keep the enemy at bay. I will keep temptations from striking you and dragging you off into captivity. Lust, fear, greed, jealousy, hatred...all the devices the evil one uses to lure My people into his traps, will always be exposed. You will be given the ability to overcome them as you walk with your hand in Mine and your eyes set on Me.

"No other scheme will keep you safe. I am the Savior of the world. Remain hidden in Me because your enemy does prowl about looking for whom he can devour. I will keep you safe. It is not a religious activity that keeps you safe; I do. Organized religion won't make you secure; I will. Many put their hope in man or in manmade institutions, but it is to no avail." (See 1 Peter 5:8-9.)

Set Your Eyes on Him Not Men

Because of my questioning gaze, He explained: "I can use men to help and inspire you, and I do, and I will; but don't put your trust in these men or in the organizations they father. Your full trust and confidence must remain in the God who established these men and their organizations to help you. If you set your eyes upon anyone or anything other than Me, you will be setting yourself up for disappointments and eventual failure. Let Me remain the source of all that is good in your life, and don't expect men to provide what I alone can.

"Don't stop Me from using men, or their organizations, from serving your needs because you fear being hurt by them. Trust Me to bring those alongside you that I have prepared for that purpose. My warning is not against them, but is against the desire within you to set your faith in them, and not in Me. Put your trust in Me alone, and you will never be disappointed. I will not let you down; I must remain your all in all."

His love and glory poured all over me as He continued: "Put your hand in Mine and trust Me to take you over all the hurdles. Yes, the path you are on is beset with many obstacles. Some are of your own making because of your insecurities and fears. Others are the direct result of the resistance the enemy has placed along your path to stop you or misdirect you to a contrary way. Still, other hurdles come from living amongst sinful men.

"And do not be surprised to learn that some hurdles, even most of them, are allowed by Me to test your prowess and your resolve to follow Me," He counseled. "As you leap over each difficulty with your hand in Mine, great strength and spiritual endurance are your portion. If you back down and stall, much damage is done to your resolve and determination; but I am able to restore your strength as you turn to Me for help in these storms of life.

"Failure can be turned into future victories, as I show you how I view each circumstance and teach you a better way to handle it. My wisdom will help you to sail over obstacles that in the past were your undoing. Bring your failures to Me and watch My resurrection power turn them around to benefit you."

> *It was good for me to be afflicted so that I might learn your desires* (Psalm 119:64).

The Hurdles of Fear

Teaching me further, He explained: "Fear of failure is a hurdle that causes many to stumble and fall. Just approaching a situation, which in the past has been your undoing, will cause many to stop and go no further. Anticipating a similar failed response sometimes causes no response. When you approach a situation in which you have suffered defeat, put your hand in Mine, lean completely on Me, and I will give you the victory. My Spirit within you will speak words of wisdom as you resist the temptation to retreat. All that you have learned from past failures will support you while you advance in the full strength of your calling.

"Remember you are not alone," He continued, giving me the key to overcoming in the midst of the storm. "Worship Me when the hurdles become insurmountable. Worship the God who puts flight to your feet. Worship the God who controls your destiny. Worship causes the height of the hurdles to suddenly diminish in your sight. Just as suddenly, the impossible becomes easily attainable. Worshiping your God is fundamental to your successful achievement of the goals that I have set before you. Nothing is outside your reach through Me. Worship, worship, worship and you will leap and dance and run. When you fall, worship and you will rise again. When you succeed, worship, and you won't fall into the trap of pride. Worship when the way is smooth and you won't forget to worship when the hurdles appear."

Practice Makes Perfect

During my next encounter with the Lord, once again, He spoke to me about the storms of life that we all encounter on the Earth. In this interactive vision, I was swimming in the river on my back blissfully looking up at the sunny sky.

I realized that the Lord was beside me and He said: "You are never alone. No matter what the circumstances are around you, I am there. If the sun is shining and all is going well, I am there. When the storm clouds assemble and torrents of wind and rain pour down upon you and yours, I am still there.

"Many times," He continued, "when all is going well, My children know I am with them, but when problems arise, they believe that it is because I have left them. This is not the truth. When the storms of life buffet you, My arms encircle you and keep you. Do not fear that I won't stand with you in the midst of difficulties, because that is when My presence can be felt more poignantly. Welcome storms as opportunities to run into My arms for safety. I am your shelter and mighty strong tower. I am your refuge in the midst of the storms of night. I can cause the bitter to taste sweet, by your trusting Me when the winds are blowing all about you. My comfort is sweet and will sustain you during the bitter battles that are common to all who dwell upon the Earth."

He cautioned, "Those that run away from Me during these sudden storms forfeit My embrace. Practice running to Me no matter what happens, and then when the violent storms arise, you will know the way to My outstretched arms of love. I wipe away the tears and will cause the sun to shine on your life once again, if you let Me by trusting Me to turn things around for you and yours.

"Circumstances don't control your destiny; I do, if you let Me through faith and trust. When the storm rages the hardest, these are the times that I can be felt the strongest, by those who rely on Me for their source. Allow Me to be your hiding place when the winds of adversity hit, and joy will come in the morning. I am a friend in all seasons, not just in times of fair weather. There are many who are only fair-weather friends, but I am not.

"Remember," He said, "practice turning to Me daily, so the way will be made smooth for you to run to Me in the darkness of the night. A well-worn path into My arms is more precious than gold. Enjoying the sunny days with Me keeps the path clear and passable during the darkness, when trials hit.

"Some say that many turn to Me only in times of difficulty, but that is not true," my Teacher warned. "If they have not made it a habit, a way of life, to sit before Me in the good times, they will not find Me when darkness falls. They may curse Me or blame Me for their difficulties, but they won't see Me in the midst of the storm. Many a fist has shaken in My face while I have stood before My hurting, angry children, extending solace and comfort. If they would but reach out to Me, and not against Me, great help and release would be theirs.

"A shaking fist cannot receive like an open hand can. Come before Me with open hands and soft hearts, and the healing and glory I long to give you will be yours."

> *Oh, that we might know the Lord! Let us press on to know him! Then he will respond to us as surely as the arrival of dawn or the coming of rains in early spring* (Hosea 6:3).

Launching Out into the Deep Burden-Free

Once again in the spirit realm, I observed myself in a vision sitting on a large rock at the edge of a very rough sea. Instantly fear came upon me while I watched the churning waters come threateningly close.

In the silence, I heard the familiar voice of my special Friend say: "Things are not always as they appear to be. What looks to the human eye to be threatening and dangerous can in fact be a blessing sent by Me. Learn to come to Me for the truth. Ocean waves, signifying change, can appear to be violent, cold and turbulent, or they can be warm, comforting and life transforming. To My children, they seem to be powerful and have the capacity to be harmful, but touched by My hand and sent by Me, these waves can bring the blessings of God to My little ones."

Sitting looking at the rough waters and the approaching waves, I saw things I had surrendered to Jesus being carried in the swirling waters. They were bobbing about, going under the water, and resurfacing over and over. The tumultuous interaction of the water on these people and concerns of mine was causing them to be changed. Rough edges were being made smooth and excesses were being rubbed off until they were perfected. The more things I truly surrendered to Jesus, the more of these items appeared in the ocean before me.

Children I loved surfaced. Many people I was close to, and had released to the Lord, began to crowd the waters. Some were laughing, enjoying their time in the rough sea; others were struggling and trying to find a way out. The accepting ones floated and basked in the sun as they rode the waves. Soon the ones that were struggling, while watching the others enjoying their ride, got the idea to accept their place in the ocean and let the water have its way with them. As soon as they did, they came to the surface and floated toward shore. To my dismay, I observed that those who were frantic and hating where they were remained in the deep water far from land.

Jesus explained, "Faith in Me, and in My ability to care for you, fuels a spirit of acceptance that makes life easier and brings success. Peace and joy abide, as acceptance fosters change."

Stay on the Solid Rock

Continuing in this interactive vision, I now saw myself walking on top of large, black rocks that were almost totally covered by the swirling water. It was then that I realized the rock that I was sitting on was not on the shore but out in the ocean. Carefully I stepped from rock to rock, not knowing where I was going or where I would end up. Meanwhile, my concerns were bobbing in the water about me.

Again my Friend explained the meaning of what I was experiencing: "This is another picture that I am giving you about life. You can remain secure and in total peace, if you stay on the Solid Rock and allow Me to lead you step by step. If you try to carry all of your burdens and don't release them to Me, then you will be unable to launch out into the deep with Me."

What I found remarkable about this vision was that, other than being with Jesus on my journey from rock to rock, I was completely alone but not lonely. Walking from rock to rock, in the distance, I noticed a very flat rock out in the sea. Eventually I reached this spacious, sunny rock in the middle of the ocean that was going to be my home for a season, and I was glad. I felt secure there with Jesus. We laughed and thoroughly enjoyed one another's company.

"Change brought about this season of tranquil rest," Jesus counseled. "Never fear change, but follow Me, though the way appears difficult and dangerous. Take one step at a time, as I lead you forward, and you will find rest for your soul. Change is good and productive when I initiate it."

All I needed was on this rock. Nothing could hurt me, and everything I required to complete my life and make me happy was provided.

Instructing me further, Jesus said: "Do not be anxious concerning tomorrow. I have led you to this place of broad streams and peaceful living. Trust Me with your future and the well-being of all you care for. Tomorrow can't escape My gaze, but let it escape yours. Keep your eyes fixed on Me. and enjoy the blessings of today without being robbed of your peace and joy, by being troubled about what tomorrow will bring. All of your tomorrows are being carried along by My grace. They have not escaped My scrutiny and are being carried to the place I need them to be, to coincide with My plans for your life. Trust Me, for I am well able."

Now I understood clearly. Everything we have surrendered to Jesus was floating or being submerged in His grace, His unmerited favor. What a wonderful truth I had seen. To give Him a treasured loved one, was to place them into the ocean of His favor and grace (see Psalm 18).

Through all of these deep spiritual encounters, my Lord taught me how to remain faithful to Him in the midst of the storms of life. When life was going well, it was easy to hear His voice and stay in His glorious presence; but when difficulties or threats of impending problems loomed over me, fear and worry often overwhelmed me. Determined to implement what He so powerfully taught me, I went on with Him to another path in life, a path that would help me defeat all fear: The way of knowing, trusting and believing in who He truly is.

> *...he goes on ahead of them, and his sheep follow him because they know his voice. But they will never follow a stranger; in fact, they will run away from him because they do not recognize a stranger's voice* (John 10:4-5).

Chapter Eight

FEAR IS A TORMENTING SPIRIT

But now, this is what the Lord says—he created you, O Jacob, he who formed you, O Israel: "Fear not, for I have redeemed you; I have summoned you by name; you are mine. When you pass through the waters, I will be with you; and when you pass through the rivers, they will not sweep over you. When you walk through the fire, you will not be burned; the flames will not set you ablaze."

—ISAIAH 43:1-2

"Fear is one of the greatest weapons the enemy uses to separate My children from Us," I heard Jesus say. Looking into the spirit, I saw myself floating on the sea of love; Jesus was standing beside me and Holy Spirit was adjacent to Jesus. They were waist deep in the calm water. Immediately, I looked for Father! I heard Father laughing, while saying that He was happy that I remembered what He told me in the past, that whenever I was with Jesus and Holy Spirit, He was always there, because They are one.

In the distance, I could see large, threatening waves, but they were not able to make the water I was floating on ripple. Love and peace were my resting place in this sea of glory and love. Contentment filled my being. Looking again at the rough sea lurking in the distance, I began praying for all those things the turbulent waters represented: the coronavirus plaguing the nations, the civil unrest and division in our land, those tormented by fear, addictions, mental illness and disease.

Father explained: "Fear is one of the greatest weapons the enemy uses to separate My children from Us. I chase fear away, whenever My children seek My help. All fear is detrimental to the well-being of My people, and the enemy flagrantly uses it in their lives on a daily basis: fear of abandonment, fear of death, fear of failure, fear of rejection, fear of eternal damnation, poverty, loss... These are but a few of his devices to gain a foothold in their lives. This is why I invite them to come daily and sit with Me. In My presence, soaking in My glory, is where the fullness of joy abides. Peace like a river flows and all fear is chased away by My words that are filled with great love—a love that inspires great faith. Remember, perfect love casts out all fear. (See 1 John 4:18.)

"Fear is a tormenting spirit the enemy uses to try to separate Me from My beloved. People whose minds are caught in the grip of fear cannot get their thoughts focused on Me and on what is good and pleasant. By fear, demon spirits rob them of the joy I delight in pouring out on them.

"Teach My children not to entertain any fearful, anxiety producing thoughts. When troubles threaten to arise, tell them to see themselves running into My arms of love where they are always safe. To know and believe My promise that I will never leave them or forsake them will give them the faith to know I am right there to embrace them, to carry them and to calm the storms that they are facing. Faith causes the rough seas to subside. Sheltered in

My arms of love, their peace, joy, hope and strength will all be restored quickly.

"Fear must be seen as it truly is: a device to rob My children of all that is enjoyable in their lives. This is why I invite all to come to Me who labor and are heavily burdened. Rest, great peace, and joy that refreshes, are all found in My arms of love."

Fear Paralyzes, Faith Conquers

"Don't fear what your enemies threaten to do to your land or to you; live and breathe faith. Yes, let faith in My goodness, My power, and My faithfulness fill your mind and heart. Never let fear come near you.

"Fear is the weapon your enemies use to defeat My people. Didn't Goliath paralyze My army with his threats? Fear paralyzes and gives the enemy the victory, if it is not conquered by champions of faith. Like David, let your hearts and minds be so filled with love and faith in Us, that no fear will stop you from advancing and conquering the giants of death, destruction and failure that threaten to destroy you and your land.

"Intimacy was David's greatest weapon. By spending long hours in My presence, he came to know well the God he worshiped and served. My bride will have the same courage, fueled by the same great faith in Me that David had. It only took one boy filled with faith to defeat the giant that paralyzed a nation; I only need a few who know, love and serve Me to conquer the enemies that are paralyzing your land and its people.

"Inspire your nation to serve us just as David did. Let the worshipers arise and sing songs of deliverance over this land, and you will see the glory of your God arise. My glory chases darkness—all evil—far away. Just as David slayed Goliath and chased the army of the Philistines away because My glory was on him, so too, in this hour My bride will chase the armies of satan far away!" (See 1 Samuel 17.)

Faith Increases as His Majesty Is Displayed

Vividly the Lord began to speak to me about who He is and how I could truly know Him by looking at His creation:

"You must know what a mighty God you serve if fear is to be destroyed in your heart. Knowing Me, in all of My might and majesty, inspires faith and confidence that crushes fear and worry. Mightier than the crashing waves of the ocean during a major storm, deeper than the depths of the ocean, higher than the mountain heights, stronger than the powerful rays of the sun: that is who I am. Nothing is greater than the God you serve; out of My majesty pour mighty works."

His soothing voice continued, "Put your hand in Mine, and expect great things of Me. Expect Me to move mountains of difficulties and destroy oceans of impossibility. Expect the impossible. Watch for the unexpected, because I am working on your behalf. Let the waves of My peace wash over you, and you will find rest for your soul and delight for your heart. Trust Me to make a way where the passage is impossible. Nothing is impossible for Me. I will perform My promises to you, because I am as faithful as I am mighty."

When I looked into Jesus' eyes I saw ocean waves, the sun shining brightly, and a mighty, explosive volcano erupting. I saw green fields dotted with flowers and snow-covered mountains reaching above the clouds, high into the sky.

"If you see so much beauty and strength in Me," He asked, "then why do so many things trouble you? Am I not able to take care of all that you place within My hands? I am competent, so trust Me with all your problems."

When I began placing things that were concerning me into His hands, I was surprised at the large number of issues that were burdening my heart.

Encouraging me, He added, "All of your fears open you up to the attack of the enemy. Peace is a shield that keeps him from touching you. As you release your burdens to Me, your shield of peace will be restored, the wall of protection back in its place, and your health restored."

Chapter Nine

Faith in His Majesty Makes Us Unstoppable

This is what the Lord says, he who made the earth, the Lord who formed it and established it——the Lord is his name: Call to me and I will answer you and tell you great and unsearchable things you do not know.

—Jeremiah 33:2-3 (NIV)

Strengthening my faith with His powerful words of wisdom, one delightful day I heard Father say: "Believe that I am a big God. Know that I created the heavens and the Earth. As you watch the sunshine in the sky, suspended in the atmosphere, along with all the stars and planets, as you gaze at all the marvels of My creation, know what a mighty God created it all. If your faith in Me remains small, then your little belief limits Me. I am a big God! If I can create the Earth and suspend it in the atmosphere, what is too hard for Me? If I possess your life fully, through your faith and absolute surrender to Me, then nothing can stop Me.

"I capture the wind and the rain and release it as I wish. I stir up the waters and cause tornadoes to form. I blow upon the mountains and make volcanoes erupt. I touch the Earth, and it opens at

My command. The Earth is Mine, and it obeys My commands. Believe in who I am, and all your fears will be destroyed. The greater your faith, the greater will be your peace."

While He spoke, in the spirit, I saw the finger of God stir the waters of the ocean, until a vast funnel formed. This deep funnel could draw islands and even mountains into it because its momentum and incredible power were beyond measure. In the next instant, I saw God breathe upon the surface of the swirling ocean, and it became still and flat. The following Scripture came to my attention:

> *"Don't be afraid," Moses said, "for God has come in this way to show you his awesome power"* (Exodus 20:20).

He explained: "What you have observed in this vision is My power to influence the natural by My touch or My breath. As you and all of My children submit your lives fully to Me, I can use My power to touch and breathe upon your circumstances. When a whirlwind or funnel is needed to engulf the situations that are out to destroy you, I will be there to act on your behalf, as you let Me through your faith. When a mountain of poverty or pain arises, just a touch of My finger will cause it to drown into the depths of the sea of My presence and My glory. Watch fear and worry succumb to the swirling waters of My touch. Watch as the influence of the enemy is swallowed up. Once I breathe upon the troubled waters of the turmoil in your life, a great calm will be restored, if you will only believe that I am a great God.

"If you picture Me as small and incapable, then you limit Me from performing My will for your lives. The greater your faith and understanding of who I am, the greater your ability will be to surrender yourselves to Me. Is anything too hard for Me?" (See Exodus 19:16-18.)

Jesus Walks on Water and Clouds

Recently, the Lord demonstrated to me His awesome power over His vast creation in a truly delightful experience we had together. In the spirit realm, I saw Jesus laughing heartily, calling me to follow Him up a very steep, tall mountain. He walked and leapt to a height above the clouds. I stood and watched in amazement as He beckoned me to come to Him. Without much effort, I was standing beside Him, looking into His eyes, viewing a massive, cloud-filled, blue sky surrounding us. It was as if the ground around us was made of soft, fluffy cotton for as far as I could see. Flying high in the sky in an airplane had not prepared me for the splendor of the sight I was now observing.

Jesus called me to leave the security of the mountain and follow Him as He walked on the clouds. With Jesus all things are possible. He rules over the natural realm. He heals sick bodies, raises the dead back to life, walks on water, multiplies a small amount of bread and fish to feed thousands, and changes water into wine. Why would I doubt that He could walk upon the billowy clouds? My sense of excitement grew, because I knew He was going to reveal something wonderful to me.

Sheepishly, I stepped off the mountain's secure ground and gingerly placed my left foot upon the awaiting cloud. To my surprise, my foot didn't sink but stayed on the surface of the translucent cloud beneath me. Bravely I launched out, using both feet now, and quickly ran exuberantly after my Friend. Jesus' smile of approval made His face shine with delight as I came excitedly over to where He stood.

Not only did we walk, run and stand upon the floor of clouds, but Jesus told me to sit and lay down on it with Him. Laughing together, we lay in the spirit on the soft, comforting clouds. This was a secret desire I had always wished for since I was a young child: to lie upon the clouds in the sky. Knowing how happy this was making me, Jesus laughed a deep, hearty laugh that contagiously caused me to join Him. Together we rolled around on the floor of the sky, laughing until tears ran down our cheeks. While I laughed, I felt burdens lifting off me.

If my Friend could cause me to roll around on the clouds, He could do anything. Nothing was too difficult for Him. The natural, physical problems I was facing had to submit to His touch, just like the clouds had to support His weight. His supernatural nature was and is far greater than the natural things that try to control our lives. Time, space, weather, health issues, money and jobs: I thought of all the things that had to submit to His supreme power and authority. What a great and mighty God I served!

"Consider all the worlds My hands have formed," my Teacher and Companion declared. "Consider the sky with the sun, the moon and the stars. Consider the Earth with its vast oceans and lands teeming with life. Consider the magnitude of My creation, and know who I am. The world submits to its Author; I do not submit to it.

"Yes, I can walk upon the clouds in the sky," He stated. "The waters of the world support Me when I command it to be so. Mountains shake and tremble in My presence. Trees shrivel up and die when I tell them to. This is the God you follow and serve. I placed the Earth in the heavens and hung the stars, each in its perfect place. The sun and the moon cannot leave the spot I have assigned to them, unless I command it."

My Friend asked: "Why would you doubt My ability to support you and sustain your life? Why would you think it a difficult thing for Me to help you attain all I have called you to do? Remember always, the natural realm obeys and submits to the authority and the power of the supernatural realm. Many times you believe the opposite. Just because your eyes see things does not give them more credence than those things that you don't see with your natural eyes. This is why I take you so frequently into the spirit realm. I am training you to see with your spiritual eyes, so your faith will grow in My power to rule over all things."

He continued, "In the vision you saw, timidly, you stuck your foot out into the cloud to see if it would support you. This was faith mixed with doubt. It was faith the size of a mustard seed. That is all you need to launch out into the supernatural; faith enough to try what appears impossible. That kind of faith brings Me alongside you, to bear you up and bring you a successful outcome. Faith always produces success, and success brings joy unspeakable and delights the hearts of those who receive the benefits of that faith."

Faith Releases His Effervescent Joy

Still laughing while lying on the clouds, I listened and learned the way of faith and enjoyed its fruits. The delight of experiencing the miraculous power of faith brought effervescent joy to me.

"In the days to come," He proclaimed, "My children will experience the benefits of such faith. Joy will fill the hearts of the recipients of this faith. Miracles produce joy in the hearts of My children. Miracles will rain down from Heaven to the Earth, in the days that are soon coming. Laughter will be heard in places accustomed to silence and sorrow. When those who were lame were healed by My touch and the touch of My disciples, they jumped for joy: running, laughing, weeping in exhilarated, enthusiastic appreciation for the love that was shown them. You will see this repeated in this hour, for it is time for Me to demonstrate My glory, My power and My authority over all things. Only believe, and you shall see the glory of your God."

Now I understood how much faith was in the size of a mustard seed. I could have that kind of faith. Stepping out into the unknown with Him was not impossible for me to imagine anymore. After all, He's a big God!

Faith Causes Us to Fly on the Wings of His Spirit

"You can either climb or you can fly to your destination," I heard Jesus say. While in a vision, I saw someone climbing a vast mountain range and another person flying on the wings of an eagle.

He explained further: "That is what faith does for you. It causes you to fly on the wings of an eagle. Easily you are able to surmount every difficulty. Faith makes the rough way smooth. Know who I am, and you will fly on the wings of My Spirit. When the Israelites began to follow Me through the desert, their faith was lacking, so the way was long and arduous and not very enjoyable. If they had embraced a lively faith in Me, the way would have been made smooth and the journey shortened. Joy would not have escaped them.

"Faith causes the mountains to be cast into the sea. Faith causes you to fly. It puts wings to your feet. Believe in Me, and you will easily surmount every obstacle the enemy throws across your path. Believe in My great power. Believe and don't doubt. Don't believe that My plans and purposes for your life will be thwarted by an enemy who is already defeated. Believe in Me, and you will receive of an abundance that I alone can deliver. All of your needs will be extravagantly supplied, if you will but believe in the glory, power and the might of the great God you serve.

"Who am I?" He asked me. "I am He who is able to perform all you can think or ask, as long as it is in accordance with My will. I am He who is unstoppable. No plan or scheme of the enemy can bring Me down. I am the creator and sustainer of all life. I am the mighty God of Israel. Once I have put My finger upon a person or a people, they are Mine, and I am well able to keep them, as long as they remain Mine. That is who I am. That is who you serve. So trust your God to fulfill His word to you, His way and in His timing. Let go of all your fears and worries and let Me act on your behalf."

> *"The days are coming," declares the Lord, "when I will fulfill the gracious promise I made to the house of Israel and to the house of Judah"* (Jeremiah 33:14).

Faith—An Act of Rest

In a wonderful prophetic encounter, during which I would learn a valuable lesson about faith, I saw myself climbing a rugged mountain. As I climbed, I passed through clouds that encircled the steep terrain. Once I walked through the clouds, I came to a grassy knoll. There I felt free and at ease. All that troubled me as I climbed the rocky bluffs disappeared, and instead, joy replaced anxious concerns for others.

While on the way, I felt my Lord's presence beside me; but now, I was able to see Him and hear Him more clearly: "Come apart with Me and rest. For I have seen you struggle and strive in prayer. I have seen you cry out on behalf of your nation and your loved ones. Now just rest and be assured that I will act, while you simply believe. Yes, faith is an act of rest."

Then I saw myself lying on a bed of thick, green grass, surrounded by flowers. The bright blue sky cheerfully hugged me, while many elegant butterflies gently landed around me. "You can stay wrapped in a cocoon of fear and worry, or by faith you can come to Me. Come where My glory resides—and leave all for Me and My angels to take care of. Bask in My love, and believe in My love for you. Believe that just because I love you—and just because I can—and just because I want to—I will act on your behalf."

> *He will command his angels concerning you* (Psalm 91:11-12).

He continued, "I will defend you and yours. I will heal all who need healing. I will deliver those held captive by the enemy. I will bring truth to those who are deceived. I will, because I can! Trust Me in this hour, and as you rest, I will act on your behalf. Yes, trust Me, for all you bring to Me: both the little issues and also the weighty matters—even the international concerns that trouble you. All you ask for, I will grant because we are one."

The Lord explained that the more we enter the spirit realm in faith and total trust, the more we would see, hear and receive. Faith was the key to enter this place of broad streams and rich pastures. This was the place where His glory dwells—the place where miracles are commonplace.

As I lay in His glorious presence, I instantly became aware of what each of the beautiful butterflies represented. Each one was a person whose life had changed, or was about to be changed, by those prayers answered by my King and Friend. No longer were they wrapped in a cocoon of poverty, fear, addictions, demonic control, sickness, etc. But now, with eyes of faith, I saw each free—touched by the Master's hand—blessed and alive with His glory. (See Zephaniah 3:14–20.)

> *If you remain in me and my words remain in you, ask whatever you wish, and it will be given you* (John 15:7).

Chapter Ten

Led by Holy Spirit to Trust

A man can receive only what is given him from heaven.

—John 3:27

One day, while walking in the spirit with Jesus, He led me to the ocean we often visited. Inviting me to come for a swim, we walked into the water and started swimming together into the deeper water. As we swam along, two dolphins came and swam beside us. Jesus climbed upon the back of one of the dolphins and told me to climb upon the back of the other. Riding alongside Jesus on these wonderful friendly dolphins, we soared through the water. Nothing could stop us, or rob us of our great enjoyment in each other, and in our adventure together.

Jesus shared His heart with me: "In the same way, you can fully enjoy your adventures in life by staying close to Me and keeping your eyes fixed on Me. I am looking for those who are diligent and dependable, because they are devoted to Us. Those who are faithful will be promoted in this hour. All others will be overlooked, until they fully and consistently embrace these qualities. It is I who promote or overlook.'

Continuing to go further out into the ocean, riding safely on our dolphin friends, we were taken to a very large ship. Arriving beside the ship, Jesus led me to a ladder that hung off its side. Together we climbed the ladder and went abroad. Looking about, I observed that this was a party ship, but at the same time, it was a mighty warship. People were relaxing on lounge chairs, swimming in the pool and thoroughly enjoying themselves.

Jesus said: "This is where we are taking you: to a place where you will find delight, relaxation and rest, as we conquer the forces of darkness together. Trust Me-trust Us-and you will live on this ship while enjoying the ride of your life. Just keep your focus on Me and not on the battle or the tasks before you. Easily, I will supply all you need, while you relax and enjoy yourself."

The Lord told me that the dolphin's name that I was riding on was Grace. Grace took me, with Jesus, through the deep, living waters of the ocean, to my destiny, where I climbed upon the ship named Trust.

Encountering Holy Spirit

Once again, a few weeks later, while back in the spirit, I saw myself on the large ocean liner, Trust, that was a luxury cruise ship and a warship, too. As I walked on the deck, to my utter amazement, I saw the Holy Spirit. He was so big and majestic, dressed in red and gold, like a mighty warrior king. With ease, Holy Spirit led me from one large, mounted machine gun on the stern of the boat, to another. I was laughing, as I took the handle of the gun and shot large demons that were coming very close to the battleship. They were mammoth and grossly ugly. Laughing the entire time, I shot each one and destroyed them. With Holy Spirit guiding me, I easily, and with effervescent joy, went from one gun to another and shot many demons that were encroaching upon the ship called Trust.

Jesus explained: "This is a true picture of what happens when you are led by Holy Spirit in intercession. More effective than you ever imagined are the prayers of those who place all their trust in Us and fearlessly fight their foes. Joy, hope, peace and total protection are the fruit that falls on those Holy Spirit is allowed to lead in each battle."

Walk in Faith

> *Is anyone of you in trouble? He should pray. Is anyone happy? Let him sing songs of praise. Is anyone of you sick? He should call the elders of the church to pray over him and anoint him with oil in the name of the Lord. And the prayer offered in faith will make the sick person well; the Lord will raise him up. If he has sinned, he will be forgiven. Therefore confess your sins to each other and pray for each other so that you may be healed. The prayer of a righteous man is powerful and effective* (James 5:13-16).

In a vision, I saw a child in a schoolyard being bullied by someone who was very imposing and violent. That person had stolen the child's backpack, lunch and belongings. Then I saw the child's father come and defend the little boy. The bully was commanded to return what he stole and told to leave the little child alone.

Explaining the meaning of this vision, my Friend showed me that our Father will do no less for us. Furthermore, our God wants us to rise up and defend the helpless by using the authority His Son purchased for us.

"Use My authority," Jesus exclaimed, "and command the enemy to release those held captive, and command him to return what he has stolen. Now is the hour for My children to receive back what was stolen from them in seasons past. By faith, arise and declare the power and might of your God. Walk in faith, not in fear. Contend with your enemy and defeat him soundly! Retrieve all. Plunder his camp and walk away blessed and enriched."

The Lord continued, "Do you believe that the great God of glory resides within your temple? Do you believe that all that I am and all that I possess are at your disposal? Do you believe that you can achieve all that My Son did while on the Earth, because you have the same Holy Spirit in you? It was by My Spirit that My Son healed the sick, raised the dead, and saved mankind from their sins. It was by My Spirit that He defeated the enemy and destroyed the works of the devil. You have that same power abiding in you. Believe!

"As you abide in Me, I abide in you. As you submit to My authority, you walk in My authority. Live in complete union with Me, and you will see the glory of your God."

> *Remain in me, and I will remain in you. No branch can bear fruit by itself; it must remain in the vine. Neither can you bear fruit unless you remain in me* (John 15:4).

Death Is Destroyed by Life

He continued teaching me how to abide in Him: "Sing My praises, listen to My words, obey My commands, walk in righteousness, sit in My presence. If you do this you will remain connected to Me, the Tree of Life. Then you will be able to impart life to others. I have called My people to be life givers, but many impart death by their thoughts, words, and actions. Stay connected to Me, the Tree of Life; and watch miracles occur when My life flows through you. Like fruit from a tree, life will pour out of you and defeat the power of death that is destroying many lives.

"Death comes in many ways. It saps life from marriages, families, finances, and vision for the future. That same spirit of death attaches itself to groups, as well as individuals. Death can destroy churches, governments and nations. The power of death must be destroyed by the power of My life—My glory—flowing through My bride.

"Like Mary bringing the Savior into the world, My bride must birth My life, glory and power. By receiving and walking in the fullness of their faith in Me, My precious ones will impart life wherever they go. Their words and prayers—when they are one with Mine—will destroy deaths' power and bring life to all—even nations." (See Ephesians 6:17–18.)

Faith-The Currency of Heaven

> *Now faith is being sure of what we hope for and certain of what we do not see* (Hebrews 11:1).

While in prayer I heard the Lord say, "Faith is the currency of Heaven. When you go to another nation or country, you must purchase their currency in order to buy what you need. The same is true, if you want to bring to the Earth those things that are stored up in Heaven. You must purchase them with the currency of Heaven. Faith is the true and only currency that we use in Heaven."

In this heavenly encounter, as we flew in the spirit in the heavens far above the Earth and beneath Heaven, I saw all that was needed on the Earth within our reach. In Heaven, I saw people receiving all they wanted and needed, simply by faith. All had an abundance of lavish homes, joy unspeakable, health and youth. None lacked for anything, because they simply believed their Father would provide it, and then they received it.

"This is the kind of faith that is lacking on the Earth," Jesus declared. "A genuine lack of trust that I will supply all that is needed exists, as well as a true lack of belief that I can do those things that will transform lives and nations. Access is denied because most lack heavenly currency. Faith in mankind, or in technology, or in one's own abilities, will not produce what you need. But faith in Me—the one true God—will bring the delights of Heaven to the Earth.

"The more you use and give away this heavenly currency, the more you will get back. Give out faith by exercising itand it is increased exponentially. For example, when My people tithe, they give Me their 10 percent, and I open the windows of Heaven and return that blessing back to them touched by My hand, blessed and increased (see Malachi 3:10–12).

"The same is true of faith. Use it, and I will touch all you present to Me in faith, and return it back to you, blessed. Give Me your sons and daughters, and I will return them to you transformed by My touch. Trust Me with all you give Me, because you know who I am, and in return, I will act on your behalf. Give Me all that troubles you, in faith, and watch what your faith will purchase—miracles!"

Then I remembered the Hall of Miracles in Heaven. All the Earth needs is held there. God has everything at His disposal, just waiting for us to come and purchase them with prayers of faith. Let us go boldly to the throne of grace and mercy and ask for those things that God is waiting to give us. Let us ask with faith for His ever-increasing glory and love and all we need for a joy-filled life!

Filled with a greater faith and a sustaining hope for my future, I was ready for another revelation, one that would help me understand how deep and how wide His love is for all.

Chapter Eleven

THE WAY OF LOVE AND TOLERANCE

The earth is filled with your love, O Lord.

—PSALM 119:64

While quietly meditating on the power and majesty of my God and allowing my faith to grow in His ability to care for me, His loving presence and great glory filled the room I was in. My spiritual eyes were opened to see an amazing vision. As in the past, I saw myself floating on my back on a river, but this time the gently flowing river turned into a torrent. The waters became so rough that I soon found myself tumbling down a massive waterfall, which quickly brought me into a waterspout. Sliding down this deep, long, watery tunnel, I landed on the floor of a dark room.

During this encounter, I was at peace and not at all afraid, because the Lord was showing me that the river represented His love for His people. I was experiencing the power of His passion for us, in the tremendous surges of the water I was immersed in. Throughout the time I was in the spirit in this encounter, Jesus beckoned me to relax and enjoy His expression of love manifesting through the river.

Once I landed on the floor of the place the water spout had taken me, I started to walk forward into a room ahead of me. In this room, I found Father sitting, waiting for me.

The Wounds of Unrequited Love

His heart was revealed, when He began to tell me His secrets; "I love all My children. I love the murders, the thieves, the immoral, the violent, the child molesters and the corrupt. I love them all, with a love that is measureless by your standards."

Then I saw a very deep hole, about which He told me, "Daughter, this hole represents a large cavity in My heart caused by unrequited love. My love for My children is so great, that when it is not returned to Me, it brings Me great pain. As your heart breaks from unrequited love, so does Mine."

While Father revealed His love for His rebellious children, I saw and understood how deeply He cared for each one. He treasured them, no matter what they had done. His love was so great for them that He understood what caused each to choose the path of sin they were on. He did not excuse them, but fully understood what made them susceptible to the weakness they embraced.

Father explained that He was giving many of His followers the gift of discernment, so they could love and understand others like He does:

"In the past some rejected My attempts to give them this gift, because they misunderstood its qualities. Discernment is not judging others or standing aloof looking at your brother with a critical eye. Discernment is the ability to see the whole picture as I see it. Those who embrace discernment see and understand why the sinner was so easily trapped and victimized by the evil that ensnared them. Discernment always births compassion and understanding. Every one of My gifts produces the fruit of love. If love is not the by-product, then it is not My gift in operation but a counterfeit."

Father told Me that though the pain of unrequited love was enormous, the joy He experienced from those who loved and served Him was equally overwhelming. Walking forward into the next chamber, I laughed wholeheartedly with Him, as I felt the explosion of His joyous laughter. The joy we give Him, by our loving devotion, pleases Him more than we could ever imagine. An indescribable desire to turn people to Him filled me, so that His joy would increase and His sorrow decrease.

His Way Brings Liberty

Days later, my Lord had another wonderful truth to bring to me, as I sat before Him. Covered in a blanket of His love and glory, I saw a vision of a very tall, rocky, jagged mountain. The mountain was extremely steep and made of sharp, grey rocks. I began to ascend the dangerous looking edifice. The Lord went before me, and He leapt from peak to peak effortlessly. As He did, He beckoned me to follow Him. On my own, I could barely make it over the first sharp rock I encountered at the base of the mountain. But as soon as I put my focus on Jesus, I began to soar over every rock until I reached His side. He was laughing, thoroughly enjoying His adventure. His enjoyment increased as I came alongside Him, and, together, we began leaping, almost flying, to the mountain heights.

Once I grew comfortable with the success I was having scaling this enormous mountain with my Friend, I turned and looked below to where I had come from. Thinking that I was alone with Jesus, I was surprised when I saw many people desperately trying to climb the rock strewn mountain. Some had given up attempting to scale it and were gathering rocks to make a cave for themselves. They were setting up their homes in the stark, bleak side of the mountain. Others were dead or were lying mortally wounded on top of large rocks that jutted out everywhere. With my eyes staring in amazement, I observed another group of people following a charismatic leader around the base of the mountain. Despite the fact that this troop of people was marching on a rather smooth path, they were getting nowhere, but in a loud procession repeatedly circled the mountain. They thought they were accomplishing a great deal because of all the noise they were making. But, in actuality, they were following a man, and none of them, including the gregarious leader, were being led by Jesus.

Continuing to look below, I saw another leader rapidly ascending the precipice. He grew disheartened, as he looked down and saw that those he was leading weren't keeping up with him. Of everyone in this rather large group, he was the only one fully focused on Jesus. Instantly, Jesus was standing beside this discouraged man, and his joy returned. The leader leaned down toward those struggling far beneath him and cheered them on. With vehemence, he encouraged them to keep their eyes on Jesus and to put their hand in His. Many did, and began to make rapid progress up the steep embankment. This man resembled Moses. No longer was he ascending the mountain of the Lord alone, but now he was bringing the masses close beside him, out of bondage, to a new liberty in a deep friendship with Jesus.

The Pool of His Presence

Then turning my attention back to where I was walking, out of nowhere, a small pond appeared. Very kindly, the Lord took my hand and invited me to go for a refreshing swim. Entering the warm water, Jesus explained that this was the sea of faith, His presence. The entire time I rested in the sparkling waters of this delightful pond, I was being bathed in His loving presence and His overwhelming glory.

While resting in His warm, gentle embrace, I began to see things through His eyes. I knew the love that Jesus had for this leader and understood the deep, passionate devotion this man had for his God. Immediately I saw others, who were wounded and had given up, and knew if they got their focus off the dire situation and back onto Jesus, they would make up for lost time and rapidly be in a new place on the mountain. Looking through the clear waters, I watched others reach a great height, look with approval at themselves and suddenly fall back to the rocky depths below. Their pride in themselves and in their achievements caused them to lose their balance and fall.

Before I entered this pool of refreshing water, I had noticed that the rocks ahead were no longer dry, but they were covered with ice. I wondered how we would ever surmount this grave obstacle. While lying in the water, a peaceful feeling enveloped me, because I knew that Jesus had it all under control. Leaving the pool of His presence and His glory, I was immediately above the ice glazed rocks and on a lush, green, grassy path I had not seen before my swim. Faith made the way where there was no way.

The altitude where I stood was so high that billowy, white clouds rested beneath the mountain path we were ascending. His presence had made the way easy. The time I thought I was losing by resting in this quiet pond actually caused me to ascend miles ahead of schedule, and with no effort made on my part.

Climbing together, Jesus and I laughed heartily as we continued on our journey.

The clouds that covered the mountain below kept me from seeing the past. In His great wisdom, Jesus wanted me to keep my focus on Him and on the path He had set before me.

> *Forgetting what is behind and straining toward what is ahead...* (Philippians 3:13).

"There is no other way," Jesus explained, "to reach the end of your course except through Me. My presence and My glory will sustain you; My encouragement will cause you to fly to great heights unhindered. It is not an occasional glance that will sustain you through life, but My continual abiding presence. The way is not easy. It is beset with many obstacles and fraught with great dangers. These can all be overcome, as you place your full confidence in Me. A surrendered life knows great joy and is guaranteed success. Pride, the most subtle of all enemies, can easily be thwarted by My presence, because I am humble and holy."

Listening to Jesus speak these words reminded me of the people I saw down the mountain. With disgust, people having jealous and hateful thoughts were sneering at their neighbors who climbed near them up the mountain peaks. Once they became engaged in this judgmental activity, they soon lost their footing and fell far below.

Jesus exclaimed, "This is why I say: Judge not; love your enemies; bless and give wholeheartedly; encourage one another! This is My way. Every other way will lead to your demise. My way is the way of love and tolerance. Come follow Me. Time spent in My Presence, soaking in My glory, is never wasted time, for in My presence is found the very fullness of joy."

When He Comes on the Scene the Enemy Scatters

A few days later He taught me about the tremendous power His love has:

"My presence is like a cool, refreshing rain on your face when the heat of trials and tribulations has grown intense. Come to Me and feel My refreshing touch and be restored. Nothing else compares to feeling My presence and My glory flowing upon you, because you are being bathed in My love. Feel accepted and cherished. Feel approved of and delighted in. Feel the love of a favored child by its parent."

He explained further: "When you feel the onslaught of the enemy coming at you, attacking you like wild animals trying to tear you apart, come to Me. Don't hesitate or focus on the fierceness of the adversary who is surrounding you. This won't help you, but I will. Come to Me. Find solace in My arms of love and let My presence drip all over you. Remember, when I come on the scene, the foe scatters."

Before I had received this comforting word, I had seen a disturbing sight in the spirit realm. It was not customary for me to see such things, but I realized that what I had experienced was a warning from my Friend and clear instruction how to handle the enemy's devices. In this very brief vision, I could see and feel the presence of demons. They looked like a pack of wild animals surrounding me, and in the spirit, I realized that they were trying to attack my lower extremities. I just ignored them and the vision ended.

The Lord showed me that it is true; the enemy does prowl around like a roaring lion seeking who he might devour, if we let him. Ignoring him, or just pretending he's not there is not the answer. Running to Jesus and allowing His presence and His glory to enfold us, is. There in His arms, we receive the strategies to scatter our adversary. The attack was directed against my legs, so I knew I could not let the enemy fill me with a spirit of fear; this fear would stop me from moving forward to do those things I felt led to accomplish. Now instead of doing nothing, I worshiped and declared God's promises for victory. (See 1 Peter 5:8-9.)

Safe in the Hidden Passage of Intimacy

"Do not fear," my Lord encouraged me, "for, as you advance into your new level, I will guide and protect you. Yes, your enemy is rearing his head against you, for he knows the plans I have for you. No matter how he tries to stop you, he can't override My words. Do not be afraid because of who or what can come against you, for I am for you and with you."

Listening to these faith-building words, I advanced higher up the mountain, climbing in the spirit realm. No longer lying on the plush, green grass that swarmed with elegant butterflies, or swimming in the quiet pool of His presence, I now trudged higher up the side of this rocky mountain.

As I climbed, rocks and debris appeared, as though they were being hurled down at me. My enemy was trying to stop my forward momentum. Discouragement and self-pity were among some of the missiles that narrowly escaped me. Fear and dread barely grazed my head, but my Savior kept me close to Him and safe from all that was launched against me.

In fact, as I continued to climb, dodging the flying articles seem to increase my strength and agility. What the enemy meant for harm worked for my good. As I climbed, the anointing I was promised rested on me, in an ever-increasing measure. The onslaught kept me more dependent upon my Friend. Minute by minute, I drew closer, until I was completely hidden in Him. Like Psalm 91 declares, I was dwelling in His shelter and resting in His shadow. The more the enemy came after me, the more I sought His presence and took comfort in His word. Even with the rocks of accusation and slander barely missing me, my peace was restored and my faith increased.

What disturbed me the most was the fact that the enemy was using other Christians to launch his attack at me. He knows that friendly fire is the most difficult to endure. My Savior and Friend understands because He suffered at the hands of the religious, too. He, too, was abandoned by His closest and dearest friends. He knows the pain, but He also knows how to readily forgive those failures. Unlike our Savior, at timeswe are the ones inflicting that same pain on others. So let us quickly forgive, so we can receive that same forgiveness when we fall short.

He explained: "This is the road to an increased anointing. There is no shortcut. All who long for more of My presence, My glory and My power must climb the same mountain and endure the same onslaught from both friends and foe. With each new promotion, the way is the same. Just stay close to Me and walk the way of love and forgiveness. Praise Me in the midst of the attack, and love your enemies. Do not lose heart, but be encouraged, for I am always with you, My friend."

His uplifting words spurred me on; "When you stay hidden in Me, not only are you safe from the fiery darts of the enemy, but you can easily advance to your destiny."

Hidden in His Arms

While advancing up the steep, rock-laden mountain, the Lord beckoned me to follow Him into a cave. This hiding place was hollowed out of the side of the mountain. Nothing could touch me there. As we sat, side by side, looking out of the cave opening, I watched as numerous rocks tumbled past. Peace flooded my being as my Friend held me close to Him. He was my hiding place, my strong tower and my refuge. Nothing and no one could touch me here, hidden in His arms. I needed the rest, because the steep ascent and the numerous attacks had left me weary and worn out. Feeling safe, I leaned back and even began to laugh, fully enjoying His presence and His glory pouring on me.

Then He showed me something that I was completely unaware of. The cave we were resting in was, in reality, an elevator built in the side of the mountain.

As I rested safe and secure, I advanced up the mountain with no effort whatsoever and heard: "The deeper and closer you get to Me, the safer you will be and the quicker you will reach your destination. Spiritual promotions are waiting for those who will find this hidden passage of sweet, intimate fellowship with Me."

Suddenly, I felt the cave stop moving upward. I looked out and no longer saw the barrage of rocks and debris flying down past the entrance. Instead, I saw the sun shining and heard the sweet melody of birds chirping a song to their Beloved. Together we walked out and stepped onto the mountain pass.

Replacing the rock strewn path was a lush green meadow. Dotted with flowers and fed by a mountain stream, this place was the place of broad streams and rich pastures. Filled with curiosity, I walked over to the side of the mountain's edge and looked down.

I watched as rocks and boulders flew down the mountainside, like rain on a stormy afternoon. This was where I had come from. Such peace and joy filled my once-wounded heart that I could barely contain my gratitude toward my Friend for rescuing me.

> *Those who trust in the Lord are like Mount Zion, which cannot be shaken but endures forever. As the mountains surround Jerusalem, so the Lord surrounds his people both now and forevermore* (Psalm 125:1-2).

Chapter Twelve

Fresh Revelations on Forgiveness

And when he had taken it, the four living creatures and the twenty-four elders fell down before the Lamb. Each one had a harp and they were holding golden bowls full of incense, which were the prayers of the saints.

—Revelation 5:8

To my dismay, while in the spirit, I observed myself lying face down on the ground. My back was covered in cuts, bruises and welts. Some wounds were very old and others had been freshly inflicted. Compassionately, the Lord came over to me, knelt beside me and asked if He could remove all the festering abrasions. Meekly, I said yes, and in one motion, His ministering angels lifted all the sores off my back. It appeared as though they were connected to a transparent film.

As soon as the wounds were removed, I was transformed. No longer was I lying prostrate on the ground. Now I was clothed in a long, white garment and was sitting at the feet of Jesus. Intrigued, I watched the angels solemnly place my wounds upon a golden altar. The offering of those sufferings was consumed in the flames from the burning coals contained in this gold embossed altar. Looking more closely, I observed that the altar was called the Altar of Forgiveness.

Pure white smoke ascended from the altar and went straight to Heaven, where different angels quickly gathered the smoke into large golden bowls. These precious, smoke-filled bowls were placed close to the throne of the Father, so they could be easily seen by Him.

Leaving the Past on the Altar of Forgiveness

Gazing up into Jesus' eyes, I listened intently to His words:

"Learn from the injuries of the past, but don't revisit the events that caused the deep wounds you have endured. You have released them to Me. Let the past be burned on the Altar of Forgiveness. Start each day with Me and not absorbed in past hurts. All you have offered to Me on the Altar of Forgiveness is transformed by My touch and will be used to benefit you and those who injured you. I will work all things out for good, as you present them to Me and place them on this altar.

"The fragrance of the burnt offerings of past wounds is pleasing to Me," He said. "As the smoke from these offerings ascends to My throne room, it is caught by My angels and placed in the golden bowls that hold the prayers of the saints. While I sit upon My throne and observe the people of the world, My creation, I see them through the midst of these offerings of forgiveness. My heart melts for My wounded children and joins with their hearts, in a unity of forgiveness and mercy."

Be kind and compassionate to one another, forgiving each other, just as in Christ God forgave you (Ephesians 4:32).

The Power of Forgiveness

My Lord explained further: "Forgiveness is a gift that I ask My people to give freely and not to withhold from any, even those who are unworthy of it. Freely I forgave all when I hung on the cross, even those who were not sorry for their sins. I forgave and then they repented. Take the first step to forgive, then watch My power fall, and see the forgiven changed forever. There is mighty power in forgiveness, especially undeserved forgiveness. Such a sacrifice bears great fruit, the fruit of miracles and the fruit of My glory.

"Don't forgive out of duty, obligation or obedience, but forgive out of love for Me. Then it will produce fruit in both your life and in the lives of those you forgive. Freely you have been forgiven, now freely forgive out of love. You were forgiven, not out of duty or obligation, but out of love, so you do the same. Love as I loved. Live as I lived. Forgive as I forgave on Calvary—freely and with abundant love. Joy will be the by-product of such love and forgiveness.

"That is why so many times forgiveness offered for any other motive than love bears no fruit and no change occurs. United with Me in love, miracles will happen when that kind of forgiveness is offered freely."

He added, "Forgiveness offered for any other reason but love for My Father and for mankind would not have produced the miraculous salvation of the world. So, few are saved because love is short, and forgiveness is not offered for love of Me."

Freely You Have Received Freely Give

In a powerful vision, once again, I saw myself beaten; my back looked like it had been slashed with a whip. Then I saw my Lord pouring oil in the wounds and comforting me as He soothed my pain:

"With the same comfort that I have given to you, I ask you to go and extend that same comfort to those who have suffered abuse at the hands of others. When no one listens or cares, I do. When all turn against you, I don't. Never will I leave you or forsake you.

"Not only will I heal the wounds of abuse, but I will mount a strong defense on your behalf. I will gather those about you who will hold up your arms, as you continue to love and serve Me and My people. Where you have endured dishonor and slander for love of Me, I will establish those about you who will honor you and help support your efforts.

"Because you have not sought vengeance, but have blessed your enemies, I will bless you and use you to bless other victims of abuse. Keeping your heart pure was essential. Teach others to do the same, and all will be set free, both the victims and the victimizers, by the sacrifice of forgiveness they lay at My feet."

He continued: "Daughter, when the winds and rain of opposition beat against you, know this; you will stand, for I am with you. You have most certainly built your life on the solid rock of faith in Me. That is a life that withstands the assault of lies, false accusations, disloyalty, contempt and abuse.

"Look at Stephen (see Acts 6: 8-15; 7). The stones that were hurled at him revealed who I am to him. In the midst of the storm, he saw Me more clearly. He loved Me more dearly. He surrendered more completely. You, too, as the attack intensifies, you will see Me more clearly, hear Me more purely, and follow Me without distraction or compromise.

"Just do whatever I tell you to do. Do not fear the disdain of men who disagree with your decisions or reject your words. Just continue to fearlessly speak what I show you and do whatever I tell you. Your reward will be the same as Stephen's—more of Me—more of My glory! Press through the crowd of opposition and disdain and run into My arms of acceptance and protection."

On Enduring Suffering

The following revelation forever changed my understanding of being hidden in God: "Allow Me to shelter you under My wings. That is what I will do if you let Me. I am the God who takes My people, for a season, into the wilderness and hides them from the wicked one. Sheltered in My arms of love, they are not only protected by Me in this place, but their wounds are healed as well. That is also the place where wisdom is imparted and where the anointing and My glory is increased. Passion and love for Me, that will sustain each one through the season of persecution, are imparted as well. All you need for the successful completion of your journey will be given to you on the backside of the desert season.

"Before Moses was sent back to Egypt, while living in the desert, he received a great love for Me, which would not allow him to quit. It was there in the desert that he grew in wisdom, patience and love for his people enslaved in Egypt. I provided and pressed into his character all that he needed to be successful.

"Nothing is insignificant. Everything works for the good of those I have placed My mark upon. I mark My faithful ones and set them apart for My purposes. Each one is equipped to succeed and must not fear their inadequacies." For it is:

> *"Not by might nor by power, but by my Spirit," says the Lord Almighty* (Zechariah 4:6).

He continued: "I, the desired of all nations, come to take you in My hand. I come to shake that which is unprofitable out of your life and replace it with My glory, as you let Me. It is the life that is submitted to Me that I can take hold of and shake and shape into My likeness. It is during those times that you sit in My presence, walk with Me, and suffer for love of Me, that I press My likeness into your life, as you let Me! As you yield your life fully to Me, I will be glorified. When My likeness appears, I am glorified and exalted.

"Sometimes the shaking can be uncomfortable. It is designed to remove all that is unprofitable out of your lives and transform what remains into My likeness. It is in the shaker that lust, fear, hatred, addictions, bitterness, criticism and slander all leave and become love. During the shaking process, the ingredients of My love and My fragrance remove the impurities and transform all into My image."

He was teaching me that staying faithful and focused on Jesus in the midst of trials reshapes us and imparts His fragrance and His glory into us, which then inundates all we encounter.

My Lord said, "In the midst of every fiery trial, soak in My presence. Then My fragrance will adhere to you and no stench of bitterness, hatred or jealousy will stick to you. Saturated by My glory, the enemy won't damage you or your reputation."

For all who have been mistreated, the Lord gave this instruction:

"I will deal with those who have dealt unjustly toward you. Just keep your attention focused on Me, instead of on those who have wounded you. I am here to soothe and comfort you. Allow My love to bathe your wounds and heal your scars. Come to Me, and let Me shelter you under My wings, where the fiery darts of wickedness can't touch you. Stay close no matter what happens, and you will stay in perfect peace.

"When you lose your peace, it is difficult to hear your God and Friend counsel you. It is in the river of peace and glory that My words will flow and bring clarity, direction and understanding. Wisdom will advise you, if you allow My words to penetrate your thoughts. When your thoughts run contrary to Mine, then you are blocked from receiving My guidance. Put on the mind of Christ, then perfect peace will fill you. Put aside those issues that concern you, and just love Me. In that love, I will meet with you. Your thoughts and Mine will fuse as one, as I return your love with Mine. Understanding will flow, where confusion and fear dwelt."

> *You will keep in perfect peace him whose mind is steadfast, because he trusts in you. Trust in the Lord forever, for the Lord, the Lord, is the rock eternal* (Isaiah 26:3–4).

Run the Race with Forgiveness

After speaking these truths to me, He continued to teach me about forgiveness. Often in the course of our lives, we are met with people who do not have our best interests at heart. Frequently, they hurl insults at us or undermine our work for God. During a season in my life, when things such as these were happening, the Lord taught me exactly how He wants us to handle those very hurtful situations.

In a prophetic vision, I saw myself running a race through a dry sandy place. There were hurdles on the path and large boulders along the way. People were hiding behind some rocks waiting for their opportunity to attack me, to stop me from winning the race. Jealousy, hatred and pride motivated them. Then I saw Jesus walk over to the boulder. He stood very tall and looked down on those who hid from me—but not Him. With a kind, loving look and a firm gesture, He commanded them to leave. Ashamed, they walked away. They knew that they had displeased Him and were sorry.

When I saw Jesus walk over to the rocks, I followed and looked at those who hated me. The Lord directed me to ignore what was going on and get back to my race. Immediately, I returned to the race, because of the urgency in His command. Obediently, I ran and leapt over obstacles on my path.

Unbeknownst to me, a large snarling wolf was waiting for me down the road, but my Lord went before me and held the wolf's drooling, fang-filled mouth closed, until I was out of danger and well past this enemy.

To my amazement, I saw those who had been chastened by the Lord put on their running clothes and join the race behind me. There was no competition or jealousy present now. Those former opponents even offered me a drink of water, to help me make my goal. Where there once was criticism and contempt, cheers of encouragement came out of their mouths.

Then the Lord spoke:

"Don't ever be afraid of failing Me or of falling short, for I will lead you step by step. I will lead you over hurdles and keep those who lurk in the shadows, or are hiding behind boulders of deception, from attacking you. I will smite them, and they will know why I have come against them—so that they will have a change of heart. Just continue to keep your eyes fixed on Me. Don't allow yourself to look for those who oppose you, because I will take care of them and you!

"When I show up on the scene, I change everything, but most especially, the hearts of those I reveal Myself to. I expose those things hidden from one's own sight. Then, once uncovered, I extend the grace needed to repent and change."

Suddenly I reached the end of the course. Instead of a dry desert place, I beheld a beautiful, plush, green valley sprawling before me.

He explained: "This is what I have in store for all those who remain steadfast. For those who keep running and are not side-tracked by revenge or anger, I will lead them, through the desert of opposition to the place of broad streams and green pastures." (See Psalm 23.)

"There is no other way to arrive at this pleasant land than by coming through the desert of opposition. As you saw, sometimes the difficulties come from your own making, by leaving the path and trying to handle situations yourself instead of letting Me take care of them. Other problems or hurdles come from the struggles that are common to man. These, too, I will help you surmount, as you place your full trust in Me. Beside these issues, there are those that occur because of the opposition from men, both friends and foes. These are the most difficult to deal with. They are best handled by love, forgiveness and surrender through prayer. Then, as you observed, the enemy, like a wolf, lies in wait, through his many devices to steal, kill and destroy or to tempt you into sin. As you keep your eyes fixed on Me, I will shut his mouth and keep you steadfast on the path to your great reward."

Advance and Conquer

Then I asked the Lord what the plush, green valley I came to at the end of my race represented.

He answered: "There are seasons in the spirit realm, just like there are seasons in the natural realm. There are dry seasons, where all you do is press forward in humility and obedience, for love of Me. At the end of each dry season, those who remain faithful, those who listen and obey, will come to a season filled with My grace, My glory—My delights!

"In this season of harvest, all you did for love of Me in your dry season will bear their fruit with a great increase: like the boy who gave his meager lunch and reaped a great reward, like the fishermen who laid down their lives and professions and became fishers of men, miracle workers, great leaders and authors (see Galatians 6:9; Hebrews 10:36).

"Come and reap, for love of Me and for My kingdom's sake. My children languish and are in need of all that your good deeds have purchased. Step into this season of harvest and pray prayers of faith on behalf of My children. Immediately, you will see the results. Launch out. Just as you had to run the race with great violence, do the same here in this new season in this land of rich rewards. Advance with faith, with boldness and with courage." (See Matthew 11:12.)

> *I do all this for the sake of the gospel, that I may share in its blessings. Do you not know that in a race all the runners run, but only one gets the prize? Run in such a way as to get the prize* (1 Corinthians 9:23–24).

I knew if I just followed my Friend's directives, not only would others reap the benefits, but I would find great enjoyment and His wonderful glory while serving Him.

Chapter Thirteen

THE BENEFITS OF BEING HIS FRIEND

Greater love has no one than this, that he lay down his life for his friends.

—JOHN 15:13

Early one morning, my Lord taught me about the qualities of true friendship:

"It is a great honor to be called My friend. Few are friends of Mine. Few spend time with Me or care about My concerns. Few want a close relationship with Me. Friends take time for one another and delight in spending time together.

"Not only do they share their good times together, but they are there for each other no matter what. When the workload increases, they are there to lend a hand. If sickness comes, they share the suffering. When lack comes knocking at the door, they give wholeheartedly to relieve the poverty of their beloved. Friends share everything! Friends put aside their likes and dislikes to align with what their friend enjoys. They share everything, even their times of rest and relaxation.

"A true friend takes such delight in the relationship, that nothing is too difficult or too imposing; a friend maintains the attitude of 'whatever'! Yes, whatever you need, whatever will make you happy, and whatever will relieve your suffering.

"A friend will stay true during times of laughter, as well as during times of great sorrow. A true friend will wipe away the tears from the brokenhearted and will listen attentively. Not only will they listen, but they will hold those things in their heart and share them with no one, unless directed to do so.

"A true friend is loyal and devoted in good times and in bad. When all desert and persecute their friend, they remain loyal. Yes, these few faithful ones will even mount a strong defense.

"A good friend will protect their companion at the cost of their reputation or even their life. No matter what others say or believe about their friend, they steadfastly believe the best, with steel-like determination. They will take a strong stand against the injustice their friend is enduring." (See 1 Corinthians 13:4-7.)

He concluded our visit with this exhortation:

"The benefits of being My friend are many! I draw near to those who draw near to Me. It brings Me great joy to delight the heart of those who love Me and are devoted to Me. When My friends are in need, I always respond with all the help they need. When they are sick, I heal them. When sorrow fills their heart, I comfort them. When they are in trouble, I always rescue them. If their reputation is tarnished by slander, I mount a strong defense. Whatever pleases My friends, I supply. I open the windows of Heaven and pour out My glory and so many blessings; they are unable to contain them. Of a necessity, they have to share them with others."

Keep Your Gaze Fixed on Him

Sitting beside my Friend on the mountain overlooking the Earth one morning, my Lord began to teach me a vital truth:

"Come to the heights with Me, for it is in the high places where I reveal My heart to My followers. If My children would follow My advice, and keep their gaze fixed on Me, then so many ills could be avoided. Being self-focused brings self-pity, depression, discouragement, suicidal thoughts, fear, self-hatred, as well as pride and deception. Magnifying one's self only magnifies one's faults and failings. Don't put a magnifying glass on your life where every flaw is accentuated.

"In the same manner," He explained, "do not keep your gaze fixed on others. For without a doubt, the enemy will magnifies both their good and bad qualities. One is as destructive as the other. One births hatred, resentment and pride, while the other brings forth an attitude of jealousy, competition, and worthlessness.

"Instead, put a magnifying glass on Me. See who I am. The more you examine Me closely, the more you will begin to resemble Me. Gaze at My forgiveness. Look closely at My generosity. Study My grace and mercy. Perceive My meekness and gentleness. Gaze intently upon My power and My wisdom. There are not enough hours in a day, or days in a lifetime to perceive all that I am. This will bring satisfaction and change that will greatly benefit you, instead of the destruction a critical or jealous eye brings.

"Take control of your thoughts, and make them subject to you. Don't let them hold you captive. Meditate on My greatness—not your own. Magnifying My goodness—not the goodness of yourself or others. Magnifying Me, My friend, and you will resemble what you gaze at."

> *...for as he thinks within himself, so he is* (Proverbs 23:7).

"I created you to be happy. You can only find true joy in Me—not in others or yourself. So look intently at Me, study Me, listen to Me, gaze at Me and your joy will be complete!"

The Lord continued to explain:

"When Peter stepped out of the boat onto the storm-tossed sea, he was able to walk on the water, as long as he kept his gaze on Me. When he turned his attention and focus onto the turbulent waters under his feet, he sank. Let that be a lesson to you and to My people. Keep your gaze fixed on Me, especially during difficulties, and your faith will sustain you. If you turn your attention off Me and place it on the situation, the people around you, or on your own abilities, you will fail."

He explained: "Faith—supernatural faith—comes from supernatural sources. Only by feeding your faith will it grow and not diminish.

"Joseph fed his faith by standing on My promises and recounting them. He kept his gaze fixed on Me and followed My ways, avoiding sin. He became a great man by being humble and totally dependent on Me. No matter how successful he was, he did not fixate on his ability to interpret dreams, give words of wisdom, or lead others. By keeping his heart free of bitterness and readily embracing forgiveness, his faith grew. Joseph's roots went down deep into the river of My presence and My glory.

"Staying connected to Me brought a depth of faith to him that served him well his entire life. Faith produced its benefits: He became a ruler of Egypt, was wealthy, happily married with children, and was reunited with his family. He lived a life of total restoration! The fruit his faith produced was abundant. Joseph got back what was stolen from him: his destiny, his family, his position." (See Genesis 37-50 for the story of Joseph.)

Being Safe in His Presence

"The forces of darkness stalk about you; but remember, you abide in My glory and My presence, so they can't touch you," I heard my Master say while in prayer one morning. I looked into the spirit and beheld a vision of Jesus and me sitting on a high mountain. A cliff was right in front of us. I stood up and walked over to the cliff's edge and saw ugly, grotesque demons climbing up the steep mountain. Some were almost to the top where the cliff was. I hurriedly went back and sat with Jesus. The demons peered over the edge of the cleft, saw me with Jesus, and shrank away, disappointed. They couldn't launch their attack against me. Discouragement, intimidation, fear, and division were avoided just by sitting with Jesus.

He explained, "Twofold are the benefits of sitting with Me and soaking in My glory. First, you have My protection—no weapon fashioned against you can prosper; and second, you can be fashioned in My likeness. While sitting in My presence, you absorbed My peace, My love, My power, My faith and My courage. My thoughts become yours. My fragrance seeps into your being. You receive the aroma of your God and not the stench of the world. Love keeps anger, judgment, and criticism far from you. Stay in My glory and My presence, and promotion, provision and protection will follow your life."

He reminded me that the more time we spend with God, the more of His fragrance adheres to us. We become the sweet smelling fragrance of our God, and His fragrance is love. When we sit before Him daily, He marinates us with the soothing oil of His love and His glory. The more often we sit with Him, the more the wonderful scent of God will pervade our lives. I proclaimed, "Lord, let others smell your goodness and your love when they meet me."

He responded, "There is a price to pay for sitting with Me—everything. Nothing can take My place—no activity, no relationships—nothing. Once you are that absorbed in My presence, you will automatically praise Me no matter what. The voice of praise calls Me and commands My attention, just like grumbling and complaining calls the forces of the enemy to your side."

The following day, once again, I saw myself sitting beside Jesus on the top of that high mountain. Demons were climbing up the steep embankment, but because of Jesus' presence they couldn't reach the top. So they began throwing grenades at me. Instead of getting up and throwing them back, I told Jesus about each one. He directed His angels to throw them back to the camp of the enemy. Each grenade represented a problem that concerned me.

Kindly, Jesus said that He would take care of my loved ones' problems, but He would also get rid of the distractions they were intended to bring into my life. All the fear, dread, and worry that the enemy planned to use to draw me out of my King's presence were going to be stopped, before they reached me. Now, because of His protecting presence and His overwhelming glory, I would not be consumed by these things, lose my peace, or be unable to hear His words to me.

With enormous love He reminded me: "Praise Me. Love Me. Draw closer when trials appear, and I will care for you. Exactly the opposite of what the enemy plans will happen. You'll hear Me more clearly and see Me more distinctly; and you will feel My presence more than before the attack was launched. Plus, all that was intended will not happen. You will be protected from every evil scheme. Draw close and trust Me with everything and everyone."

As I watched this interactive vision, I saw angels picking up grenades that had been thrown at me from a distance below. Each angel removed the pins, which I knew were the only part of the grenade that held any truth in it. Then they placed the pins in Jesus' nail-scarred hand—where He purchased the power to overcome the works of the devil (see 1 John 3:8). All that was put in His hand was taken care of by Him, His way, and no longer were they my problems to hold onto or to worry about. Now, by faith, all had been surrendered to Jesus, just by telling Him about my problems. Immediately, as each problem appeared, I trusted Him completely and continued to remain at peace. All of my attention remained on Him—loving Him, worshiping Him alone.

Strategic Prayers

Sitting on our seat overlooking the cliff where demons had appeared days earlier, my Friend told me:

"In this place of intimate fellowship, not only are you protected and are your problems solved, but in this place of sweet surrender and loving fellowship, I can whisper My prayers to you. Those Holy Spirit inspired prayers, that are My perfect will, shall be given to you to pray." I saw His smile and heard His laughter. It spoke of victory and sweet success.

"Those are the prayers that few pray because the price is too high for most to pay. Alone for hours, soaking in My presence, is where the treasure of My strategic prayers is found. Those prayers will always bear immediate fruit, because they are Mine." (See 1 John 5:14-15; James 4:2–3.)

Before we parted He said: "Few things are black—all evil, or white—totally good. But in most issues you will see gray—a blending of the two—good and evil. Address and confront that which is evil, as I lead you. Yes, nurture that which is good and encourage it to grow. Do not ignore evil, because that which is ignored grows like weeds in a garden. If left to themselves, they will grow and overtake that which is good and sown by My hand into My children's lives. Jealousy and contempt, if left unchecked, will grow and destroy all that is good. All the love, humility and service to others will be smothered, until all that is left is of the evil one.

"Nurture the good gifts and talents in others with words of encouragement and prayers, so that they will grow at a faster rate than the weeds of contempt and jealousy, but to just ignore the weeds will not benefit anyone. As the Son of Man spoke out against jealousy and contempt, you do the same. There will be those, like Nicodemus, who will listen and attend to those warnings." (See John 3:1–21.)

Chapter Fourteen

WISDOM: THE GREATEST GIFT

If any of you lacks wisdom, he should ask God, who gives generously to all without finding fault, and it will be given to him.

—JAMES 1:5

While sitting before my Lord, I heard:

"Wisdom is the greatest gift I give My children, and so few ask for it, or seek it. Wisdom knows My will, My ways, My ideas, My plans for the future, My blueprints. If My children, who are called by My name, would seek hard after wisdom, I would grant it to them. Wisdom would change their lives, transform their businesses, and rebuild all that was destroyed in the past. Wisdom brings success and wealth and instructs those who receive her how to handle that wealth and success.

"Wisdom doesn't leave those who receive her. No, she stands beside them, gives them careful instructions and guides them in the best way they should go. Seek wisdom. Seek My will and My plans for your life, and you will receive abundantly of all I have.

If you do, then you will know how I would handle every situation you encounter." (See Romans 11:33–36.)

"To know what to do," Jesus counseled me, "and not have the courage to implement it, will bring a great frustration. So when you pray for wisdom, also pray that I will fill your heart with the courage to carry out what wisdom declares is right. Love, too, is necessary; so pray for love to overshadow all that you do or say. A rebuke spoken in love will lead to repentance; but a wise word, spoken in anger or haste, will bear no fruit."

From His wise instruction, I understood that in order for wisdom to be effective, it must walk hand in hand with love. Wisdom, along with the courage to implement God's will and words, guided by love, will transform situations.

> *If I have the gift of prophecy and can fathom all mysteries and all knowledge, and if I have a faith that can move mountains, but have not love, I am nothing* (1 Corinthians 13:2).

The Lord concluded this teaching on wisdom with this admonition: "Pray for wise leaders. Pray for wisdom, courage and love for all of your leaders."

> *The wicked man flees though no one pursues, but the righteous are as bold as a lion. When a country is rebellious, it has many rulers, but a man of understanding and knowledge maintains order* (Proverbs 28:1-2).

The Storms of Life

> *I guide you in the way of wisdom and lead you along straight paths. When you walk, your steps will not be*

> *hampered; when you run, you will not stumble...Let your eyes look straight ahead, fix your gaze directly before you. Make level paths for your feet and take only ways that are firm. Do not swerve to the right or the left; keep your foot from evil* (Proverbs 4:11-12, 25-27).

One morning, I heard the Holy Spirit speak to my heart, "I ask you, like I asked the prophet Jeremiah, 'What do you see in the spirit?'"

Obediently, I looked and beheld a great wind blowing and a bird trying to fly into the wind. This bird was determined to go in that forward direction. No matter how many times the wind overwhelmed the bird and caused it to fall from the sky, the bird got up and resumed its vain attempt at flying into the wind. The procedure the bird was enduring was very costly to it. Feathers were falling on the ground, and the bird was quite bruised from crashing so many times.

"My children," Jesus said, "learn a lesson from the bird. Fly on the wings of the Spirit, not against the direction He is blowing." Then He asked, "Now what do you see, My child?"

Once again, I peered into the spirit realm and saw another bird. This bird was very happy. It was flying high above the contrary winds. As it flew, it caught the wind and glided with it. The direction of the wind varied. As soon as the wind changed direction, the lighthearted bird flew in that new direction. If birds could squeal with delight, I knew I would hear loud squeals coming from this happy bird. Unlike the other bird that was flying against the wind, this one was completely carefree.

Again, the Lord explained the meaning behind what I saw: "When you encounter crosscurrents in your walk with Me, rise above them. Fly to My waiting arms. As you saw in this vision, the little bird was not affected by the swirling winds below him. He glided about the sky, basking in the warm rays of the sun. Learn from this bird to bask in the light of My glory and enjoy My presence. Be sensitive to the direction My Spirit is moving in. The minute the little bird felt the warm comforting wind of the Spirit, it immediately changed directions and flew on the wings of the Spirit. Take note, I will change directions frequently just like the wind does. Be ready to fly with Me and not against My leadings. Flying contrary to Me only produces frustration and pain."

He continued: "Did you notice that the bird you saw was alone? The direction I lead you in will not always be the same route I lead others. Try the winds and determine which is My path for you. That is why it is so important to know Me. Your life can be a comfortable journey, riding along on the wings of My Spirit and cloaked in My glory, or a disaster, filled with pain and grief. If you know Me and are sensitive to My Spirit, it will be a great delight and an easy matter to find the way I am leading you."

Encountering an Unexpected Storm

Yet again, I witnessed the same bird flying in the spirit, and a huge black cloud was coming toward it. "If you continue to ride on the wings of the Spirit," He taught me, "I will warn you of approaching danger. So many problems could be averted, if My people would allow Me to guide them. If they let Me, I would lead them in a direction away from troubles. Storms on the horizon would not affect them, because they would be able to observe them from a distance and not be attacked personally by them."

Thinking back on the times when I had encountered storms, or difficulties, in my life, I wondered how many of them I could have avoided if I had been obedient to the voice of His Spirit instead of blindly going my own way.

> *Then the Spirit lifted me up and brought me to the gate of the house of the Lord that faces east...*(Ezekiel 11:1).

Led by His Spirit into the Wind

One morning, awakened by the familiar presence of Jesus, joy immediately filled my heart. Instinctively, I knew that my Friend was going to bring me on another spiritual journey. I later found out that He was going to reveal to me that not every wind or experience in life is a wind reflecting the guidance of His Spirit.

As the vision unfolded, I saw myself walking through a blinding windstorm. Butterflies and other insects were flying, with the wind, at me. All alone, I was walking directly into the wind. After pushing and pressing myself forward, I finally made it through, where there was no wind and all was still. I looked behind me and saw the wind continuing to blow. Everything and everyone was traveling with the wind; I was the only one that headed into the wind. It was a wonderful feeling to get to the other side, where there was a great calm. A feeling of warmth and well-being filled me.

Jesus began to speak, "Press; press through the elements that rage about you. Don't let circumstances and ease dictate the way you go, but let My Spirit be your guiding star. If you are tossed about by every wind that blows, you will not remain steady on the course that I have set for you to travel. Many contrary winds will blow to try to stop your forward momentum, but you must resist the temptation to take the easy way out and go the way of the crowd. You must follow Me, not others."

He continued: "Many times I send the wind to test your prowess and your determination. As you push through the difficulties, My character is being forged into yours. Whenever you complete the course set before you and overcome all the obstacles, victory is sweet. The harder the winds blow and the stronger the currents are that try to pull you, the greater the sense of satisfaction you will feel when you arrive at your destination. Though the winds blow and buffet you, keep your eyes fixed on the goal set before you. Press through all difficulties and push through all distractions, and you will reach the promised land of accomplishment.

"Many times you will look back and see those who have taken the road of ease, but that is not the way I have assigned for you. The beautiful butterflies flying at you in the wind you were pressing against represent things that are beautiful and enjoyable which are not going the same way you are. Don't let these pleasant things pull you along with them, for yours is a different path than most."

The Last Leg of the Journey

The following day the Lord brought me, once again, into the spirit realm. In this vision, Jesus was walking briskly up a steep, rocky mountain that had a very rough terrain. I was following Him, trying very hard to keep up with His rapid pace. When we reached the top of the mountain, the view was breathtakingly beautiful. Flowers of every kind filled the sumptuous field that lay before us. I realized that if I had not pressed hard after Jesus on the last leg of our journey together, I would never have arrived here, and it was so close, just over the top of the hill.

He explained, "This is why I say 'press.' Do not grow weary in well doing, for before you know it, you will receive the just reward for your labors. If you grow faint and allow the enemy to take the wind out of your sails, through discouragement or slothfulness, you will be like a runner who quits the race just as he approaches the finish line. Sometimes the last leg of the journey appears to be the most difficult, but press, and your reward will be great. Don't give up, because I go before you to make the way possible. If need be, I will carry you on My shoulder, if you stay close to Me. The riches and rewards of faithfulness will completely delight you. My great glory will be your portion!"

> *I will go before you and will level the mountains* (Isaiah 45:2).

Complete Surrender Brings Victory

As He had promised me, the next time I went into the spirit realm I saw Jesus carrying me like a little child on His left shoulder. On His right shoulder sat those people I was concerned about. In His strong hands were issues and problems that worried me as well. I was laughing and enjoying the special place I was afforded, being carried by Jesus. Nothing concerned me, because He was in complete control, and I trusted Him. Jesus spoke to my heart:

"There is no better place to be than with Me. The more you trust Me and completely surrender all to My care, the more I am able to act on your behalf. When you worry, your fear ties My hands and keeps Me from acting. It is your faith and trust that releases Me to act and brings your life in conformity to My perfect plan for you. Your happiness is ensured when I am in control. Remember, I created you to be happy. Release Me by your belief in Me.

"My heart's cry is for you to be made complete in Me. It is My will for you to have complete peace, complete joy, complete love, complete faith and hope. Little bits of Me won't satisfy you. Because you were made for Me, I alone can fulfill the longing in your heart. All these issues that concern you will never produce the joy and the peace you think they will, apart from Me. If you possessed all the treasures in the world and had the total acceptance of mankind, your soul would not be at peace, because you were made for Me. If you have none of the former, but possess Me alone and have My glory, your joy would be complete.

"John the Baptist is a perfect example of this principle. His relationship with Me carried him through poverty and persecution with peace, joy and love. He was complete in Me. No man and no thing possessed him because I did. The more you are Mine, the less troubled you will be by the circumstances you face. See through My eyes. See yourself possessed by My love and carried by Me, My child. I am your great comforter, your strong tower, your Prince of Peace. I am the stabilizer in the storms of life and the bearer of good news."

I saw myself laughing hysterically as Jesus carried me through life. This was the truth: all my burdens were His. I was free to enjoy my life through His care, like a child carried by his devoted father. No longer was I running behind Jesus up the steep mountain of my life, but I was riding high on His shoulder laughing gleefully, as He leaped and bounded up the rocky path to the crest of the mountain.

Jesus lovingly summed up the qualities of faith:

"This is what faith does, daughter. It makes all things easy and enjoyable. As you release all your cares to Me, because you trust Me with them, your joy will be made complete. Fear and worry delay My ability to act quickly on your behalf. Faith brings speedy results."

...the one who trusts will never be dismayed (Isaiah 29:16).

A Holy Spirit Carpet Ride

While in prayer one morning, I saw myself in the spirit, going on a magic carpet ride with Jesus and Father. I knew Holy Spirit was the carpet. We were laughing and thoroughly enjoying ourselves as we road over the world. Occasionally, we stopped to minister in different regions. I knew that, as we flew over many areas, these lands represented the nations and people I had reached through the media.

Jesus held my hand in His and explained: "We want you, and Our sons and daughters like you, to look at your life like you are on a 'Holy Spirit carpet ride.' Don't dread where We will take you, but know that, just as enjoyable as a 'magic carpet ride' is, do We want your life to be. Don't fear falling off, because We are here with you, taking you on your life's journey to fully accomplish your purposes immersed in Our glory. Yes, there are many things We are planning on doing with and through you, but We want you to enjoy the ride of your life. If you focus on what might go wrong, it will rob you of your joy and your peace."

Chapter Fifteen

Enjoying the Ride of Your Life

Do not grieve, for the joy of the Lord is your strength.

—Nehemiah 8:10

As He had so frequently in the past, the Lord came to me in the spirit through a great outpouring of His love. Gently, He prodded me to go for a walk with Him. Saturated in His mighty love, we walked to the mountain place He had brought me to before; the place that has the large stone seat on it.

As we sat enjoying one another's company, at the spot that overlooks God's kingdom, a large, white eagle flew to the left of us. Almost immediately, this majestic bird landed on the ground beside us. Its size amazed me. Standing as He spoke, Jesus told me that we were going for a ride on this huge friend of His. Eagerly I climbed on the eagle's back, and to my great delight, I found Jesus sitting behind me. He explained that He was my rear guard and that He was protecting me from the fiery darts of friendly fire.

The white eagle was strong and majestic, but at the same time, gentle and kind like a dove. Like a child, I buried my face in his soft, elegant feathers. To my amazement, love filled these white feathers. I felt like this eagle understood all the things that concerned me.

As I lingered, with my face comforted by the velvety feathers, I heard: "I understand; I understand; I understand all that troubles you. I know you fear your own weaknesses and your inability to accomplish the things that burn within your heart to do for Me. I understand the frustrations you feel. Come with Me, and I will show you how small all these problems are in the sight of My majesty."

Flying through the spirit realm was so real that I impulsively hung on for dear life. Jesus sat behind me, with His arms extended to His sides, thoroughly enjoying the ride. While the wind blew against Him, He laughed heartily and encouraged me to sit up with Him so that I could fully enjoy the ride on this wonderful, white eagle.

My fear of falling was causing me to lean over and hold tightly. This was not giving me the freedom I needed. Carefully I let go of the great eagle's strong neck and sat up straight. Once I sat up, I leaned against Jesus and extended my arms out to the sides, just like He was doing. The wind was warm as it blew against me. Laughing so hard that tears came to my eyes, I began to realize that my Friend was teaching me a valuable lesson, one that I would not quickly forget.

Leaning over He whispered in my ear: "This is how I want you to go through your life. Trust that I am behind you and that I will keep you from falling. As you relax and enjoy the ride you are on in your life, you will feel the warmth of My presence. Freedom brings its own reward. You cannot experience My freedom if you walk in fear. Fear will always limit your ability to enjoy your life. Wherever you are going, picture yourself flying with Me behind you, and you will enjoy yourself. Fear of falling or failing will not concern you. Every experience in your life can be enjoyable, if you see Me with you in it."

I started to look at many of the situations that were troubling me: Decisions I was weighing, changes I was awaiting and projects I was trying to accomplish. After this flight in the spirit with Jesus, I realized I was not enjoying any of these events because I was so fearful of the results. I was going through them with Jesus, cloaked in His glory, but not in the manner He was showing me. I had no freedom, just fear. I was holding on for dear life, burying myself in Him, not relaxing in total trust and enjoying the ride of my life on the wings of His Spirit.

The Power of the Fear of What Might Happen

The Lord brought this truth home to me even more clearly months later, when I heard Him say, "Don't let fear of what might happen stop you."

With that warning, He asked me to follow Him up a narrow path on a high cliff that overlooked the ocean. Enormous waves crashed against the side of the mountain. Jesus was walking quickly with great determination and purpose. When I saw the waves pummel the rocky mountain, so dangerously close to the path we were on, I became reluctant to continue following Jesus. I was well aware that there was a very real danger of being pulled off the narrow path into the ocean far below.

Turning and looking at me, He said, "Don't let fear of what might happen stop you. When I ask you to follow Me, have faith in Me and know that I am in charge of the elements around you."

Reaching out His strong, steady arm, He lovingly called me to come closer to Him. I knew He wanted me to come and hide under the shelter of His arm. Responding quickly, I ran close to Him, and all the fear that had begun to paralyze me instantly left. Instead of feeling afraid, I became relaxed and joyful. Fear of the looming waves left, because I was convinced that Jesus wouldn't let them come too close. He was in charge of them, and my Friend wouldn't let them destroy me. No longer did I see the threatening, powerful waves. Now all I saw was Jesus smiling at me with a look of great love and approval gleaming from His face. I felt so loved and safe. Being close to Him brought delight to my soul and replaced the fear I felt when I followed so far behind. Gently He spoke:

"This is why I encourage My people to walk in intimate fellowship with Me. The closer each one is to Me, the greater their peace and joy. When you walk at a distance, fear can easily overwhelm you. Once you put your eyes on Me and draw close to listen to My words, you will see everything differently. Remember, I will be in complete control of your life, if you let Me. Nothing can harm you on My holy mountain of intimacy. No matter how bad the circumstances, watch Me turn everything around for your good.

"Come, there is much to be done in this hour," He continued, "let us go and be about My Father's business. The time is drawing to a close. You cannot allow the enemy to stop you and keep your eyes fixed upon those things that could happen. Instead, stay close to Me and I shall help you to see what will happen. My plans for you are good, to build you up and not to tear you down. Don't be afraid, be Mine instead. Did I not call you to follow Me on this path? You did not decide to go this way, but I directed you here. Now trust Me to bring you safely past the dangers, to the places I need you to go, where the work My Father has assigned you to do can be accomplished through His glory."

Don't Be Stung by Unsuspecting Dangers

On another occasion He showed me how to avoid certain dangers so I would be able to more fully enjoy my life on the Earth. In the spirit realm, I saw a beautiful field full of colorful flowers, a massive garden and a display of great splendor! With every step, I reached out and touched the delicate, fragrant blossoms. As I walked through the garden accompanied by my Friend, I saw bees. Jesus warned me to be careful:

"Everything is not as it appears to be. Subtle dangers are hidden within the beauty life presents to you. All is not as it appears to be. A smiling, welcoming person may actually have hidden agendas with schemes to harm you. If you continuously walk with Me, I will show you the beauty in every person you meet, but I will also warn you of any dangers. You will know the potential in every situation to harm you, if you keep your eyes fixed on Me and are not allured away from My care. My desire is that you enjoy the garden of your life, but are not stung by unsuspecting dangers lurking about undetected."

Cautioning me, He added: "The strong feeling that you get that someone means to harm you is not suspicion, but it is a warning from My Spirit within you. Listen and step away from the danger. Do not continue along the same course but let Me lead you down a different path. If you listen and let Me lead you, I will take you to a garden where the wind of My Spirit has swept the path clear of all hidden dangers."

In the spirit, I saw a strong breeze blow over a section of the massive, voluptuous garden. All the bees that flew about the flowers in that region were blown away, making this section safe for me to explore. His glory was making the way for me.

"Listen to My warnings," He said, "and put your hand in Mine. Let Me lead you past dangers to the place of safety and joy, for I would have you walk in wisdom and keep you safe from the unrelenting sting of injustice."

> *My purpose is that they may be encouraged in heart and united in love, so that they may have the full riches of complete understanding, in order that they may know the mystery of God, namely, Christ, in whom are hidden all the treasures of wisdom and knowledge* (Colossians 2:2-3).

HIS GLORY WILL TRANSFORM THE FUTURE

Let the prophet who has a dream tell his dream, but let the one who has my word speak it faithfully.

—Jeremiah 23:28

Chapter Sixteen

Called to Speak His Words

What I tell you in the dark, speak in the daylight; what is whispered in your ear, proclaim from the roofs.
—Matthew 10:27

For many years, I have prayed as an intercessor for our nation. Knowing that God alone is our hope, I have cried out for His intervention, fervently praying that our nation would return to Him. During these times of sweet fellowship, the Lord spoke to me about the future of our nation—even the world. I have kept a careful record of those prophetic words. This section of *The Glory of God Revealed* is filled with the heart-rendering disclosures I received about our nation and the future, while sitting before Him.

Whom shall I send? And who will go for us? (Isaiah 6:8).

Equipped to Hear and Release His Words

This is the one I esteem: he who is humble and contrite in spirit, and trembles at my word (Isaiah 66:2).

Spending time with my Lord has become my lifestyle. Just hearing Him and being bathed daily in His glory has filled my heart with deep satisfaction. During one of our encounters, He said very clearly:

"Yes, you have felt Me call you to the special place of putting your head upon My heart. As John laid his head upon My chest (at the Last Supper) and heard the secrets held in My heart, so, too, all who position themselves with their ear pressed to My heart will know My secrets.

"When you long to know Me, not only will I reveal My glory to you, but I will reveal what the future holds as well. Let Me show you what I think and feel about different situations. In this place of sweet communion, I will reveal the concerns of My heart to you." (See John 13; 23-27.)

The Work Is His

> *Remain in me, and I will remain in you. No branch can bear fruit by itself; it must remain in the vine. Neither can you bear fruit unless you remain in me. I am the vine; you are the branches. If a man remains in me and I in him, he will bear much fruit; apart from me you can do nothing* (John 15:4-5).

When I read this very familiar verse, I saw clearly how important it is for His spokesmen to know Him in order to speak for Him. To reinforce this truth He said,

"I do reveal Myself and My thoughts to all who seek to know Me, not just know about Me, but truly know Me. Begin with intimacy with Me, and you will finish well. You will find whatever you need in Me, in My chambers of love. Sit apart with Me, frequently."

Finally, He addressed one of the greatest stumbling blocks to our being used as His mouthpieces: His watchmen cannot care what anyone thinks about them. Courageously, they must speak, for His glory's sake and for the good of His children; always remembering that we are our brothers' keepers!

He concluded by exhorting me with this encouraging reminder for all who will accept the call to be used as His mouthpiece:

"Don't chase after men's approval, for it is fleeting. My approval is constant. I do approve of you, My friend. I approve of your desire to serve Me and speak on My behalf. I approve of your worship. I approve of your love for My people. Most especially, I approve of your love for Me. Do not fear the disapproval of men, when you have the best—My approval. I have seen your sacrifice, and I do approve of it. What else do you need when you have My favor and approval?

"Look at My disciple and friend, the Apostle John. He had my approval; though he was exiled to the deserted island Patmos. By men's standards, he appeared to be a failure, but in My eyes—triumphant! He was able to see and hear from Me. Because he delighted so much in My favor and approval, what men did to him or said about him mattered very little. This is overcoming love."

With these exhortations, my Friend prepared me to see, hear and share what He was about to reveal to me about our world and about the future. I understood that unless I knew Him well, by spending time alone with Him daily, I would not be able to hear clearly or discern purely what He desired to disclose to me about what the future holds or what the warnings are that He wants to give to His children.

In the days ahead, He revealed many things to me about the future. Some revelations are wonderful and even glorious, while others were frightening disclosures of what the enemy has planned to bring into our lives, if we don't turn to God and pray.

> *If my people, who are called by my name, will humble themselves and pray and seek my face and turn from their wicked ways, then will I hear from heaven and will forgive their sin and will heal their land* (2 Chronicles 7:14).

Chapter Seventeen

Compromise Kills

Because of the increase of wickedness, the love of most will grow cold, but he who stands firm to the end will be saved. And the gospel of the kingdom will be preached in the whole world as a testimony to all nations, and then the end will come.

—Matthew 24:12-14

A few years ago, the Lord met with me and told me that difficult times were coming to the world. Since He spoke this solemn warning, we have endured a pandemic, civil unrest and political corruption. His words revealed His heart and His desire is always for souls. There is much work to do for the hour is late!

"There are difficult times coming to your nation and to the world," Jesus solemnly declared as we sat side by side on the mountain of intimacy.

He continued: "The vats of wickedness are overflowing. That wickedness is spilling out over the entire land. The enemy's henchmen are reaping souls destined for evil.

"But at the same hour, the vats of righteousness are overflowing. I have released My angels to harvest souls ripe for My kingdom. I am calling My children to work alongside My angels and bring in a great harvest of souls, for the hour is late. Yes, the hour is at hand for souls to be reaped. All can choose freely where they will go and who will reap them."

With great sadness in His voice He explained why He is calling us to help Him:

"Many have chosen to go the way of the wicked. It is to these who are straddling the fence of indecision that I am sending you to. Bring My convicting words to them. Do not hesitate, but freely and forcefully speak whatever I tell you to say. Do not hold back the truth, for it is hearing and believing the truth that will set the captives free. Many will choose to leave the path of evil and turn to Me. Do not be discouraged at the enormity of the task before you, for I will lead you. I will speak to you, and I will perform miracles that no man can deny. Hearts will soften and turn totally from evil to Me. Trust Me for the few who won't listen, receive or turn; trust Me to chase after them My way.

"Compromise holds back My glory from being poured out. Attack compromise with the truth and expose its ability to destroy and rob My children of their inheritance. Walking a walk of compromise, one minute for Me and the next for the enemy, is walking a path of destruction. I will not pour My Spirit out on a place that houses a spirit of compromise."

He declared, "Holiness and righteousness are the order of the day. They will bear the fruit of My great glory wherever they are found. This is the hour of the great outpouring of My Spirit. My Spirit searches for hearts that are truly Mine. That is where My Spirit will be found."

From our time together, I learned that the Lord is calling those that know, love and serve Him to help Him gather in the end-time harvest. He could do this great work alone, but it is part of His delightful plan to include us. Together with His wonderful Holy Spirit working through us, we will be well equipped to lead many out of a lifestyle of sure destruction onto a new path; a path that will bring them into a relationship with their God. The laborers are few. Let us join in this glorious work for the sake of His kingdom.

The Weeping Savior

"Do not fear anything!" I heard the Lord say. "Believe that I am well able to do all, because I did it all at Calvary. I purchased all you need to live your life to glorify Me totally." Then I looked into the spirit and saw tears streaming down Jesus' face.

Shocked at what I saw I asked, "What is wrong, Lord? Why are you saddened?"

This was His startling answer:

"I look throughout the Earth to find those who love Me, place their trust in Me and truly follow Me. There are few. Instead, I see many who profess to be all Mine. They are not; rather, that is the furthest thing from the truth. They follow their own selfish desires and are led by their flesh, not by My Spirit. I weep not because they have disappointed Me, but I weep because I am saddened that they suffer because of their sinful choices. I died so that they could live full, happy, free lives. Because of their sins, they live in bondage: restricted, demeaned, poor and deluded. Foolishness fills their hearts, I don't!

"For love of My Father and mankind, I suffered a cruel torturous death. I suffered once so mankind would not, but instead of fully partaking of My benefits, so painfully purchased, they run after the enemy and embrace his ways.

"Tell My children that it is never too late to turn fully from evil. It is never too late, while they live on the Earth, to turn to Me and really embrace Me as their Savior and Lord.

"So many call Me Lord, but I am not Lord over any area of their lives. They are the lord of their lives, their thoughts and their actions. They do not do what I ask, nor do they consult Me about what I want them to do. They live disconnected from Me, yet they think I am their Lord. All the benefits of My lordship are not the theirs. That is why I weep.

"If I could be their Lord, then I would give them all I purchased on Calvary: freedom from sin, eternal life, healing, deliverance from the propensity to sin, total forgiveness and every curse broken off their lives. I weep, as I watch those I love and died for, suffer needlessly!" (See Isaiah 53.)

I whispered in His ear, "Lord, I want to put a smile on your face by letting the Holy Spirit use my life to turn people truly to you and away from sin."

He continued to speak sorrowfully: "Compromise destroys more lives than blatant rebellion. It is subtle like the fate of a frog sitting in a pot of cool water placed over a fire. As the temperature rises, the frog adjusts and does not realize that his death is imminent. The same is true of the fate of those who compromise with sin. Just a little lustful look, a small tidbit of gossip, a few wrong companions, a little drunkenness, just a couple of illicit drugs, only an occasional angry outburst, a few curse words launched at others: all are excused as inconsequential—doing no real harm. In truth, they are a trap set by the enemy of their soul to destroy them.

"The trap has been set by a spirit of compromise, and the bait must be rejected, then My children will be equipped to live joy filled, successful lives. Instead of falling into deadly traps, they can walk with My Spirit on the path of freedom and success!"

Return to Him

While reflecting on these warnings and exhortations to avoid compromise, I pondered the fate of our country. The USA was once a nation that was a son of God most high. This nation was so devoted to God that its founders crossed the ocean at great peril, for love of God, to establish a country where Jesus could be worshiped freely. No other nation can boast such claims. We are also a nation that has tasted what is good, the presence and favor of God, and spurned it.

We have been like the rebellious son in the Parable of the Lost Son who asked his father for his inheritance (see Luke 15:11–32). Not long after he got what he wanted, he left his father and his values, took all he gave him, and squandered it on wild living. After he spent his wealth and was destitute, he returned to seek the help of his loving father.

> *But while he was still a long way off, his father saw him and was filled with compassion for him; he ran to his son, threw his arms around him and kissed him* (Luke 15:20).

The Lord explained the significance of this parable further:

"Now is the hour for the USA to turn back to Me. I stand and wait with open arms to embrace and restore all: The squandered inheritance, the honor and respect of a son of God, the authority I hand to Mine, the privileges of the favored child, the signs and wonders My Spirit affords those who belong to Us.

"In this hour, I am going to pour out My Spirit, so the prodigals and the reprobates will turn to Me. I am calling the USA to return to Me. Many will respond and will turn from a lifestyle of sin, and I will throw a party—a divine celebration. My Holy Spirit will be the guest of honor. He will be presented and accepted. This will cause a great turning—a turning away from evil back to Me and to My courts. My ways will be accepted and followed with loving devotion. The poverty and lack of this current season will explode into a time of great prosperity; because wherever I am, blessings arise."

He continued, "I need you, My people, like I needed Jonah to reach the lost and to bring My message to Nineveh."

Then He promised, "I will speak through you, My children, heal through you, and deliver those held captive by the enemy as you proclaim My words. Do not fear failing Me, for I am here to uphold you." (See Ezekiel 33:1-20.)

"As Jonah was a sign of My Son being held for three days in the belly of the Earth, so too is Jonah a sign of those who are called to bring in the end-time harvests by the power and anointing of My Spirit. A whole city repented and turned to Me at his preaching. In the same way, whole cities and nations will turn to Me at the preaching of My words by the common man. Yes, Jonah was of no significance, but he was a common fellow called and chosen by Me to bring a message to Nineveh, an evil city. It was not Jonah that turned that city from sin, but it was My Spirit speaking and acting through him that performed this miraculous work." (See Jonah.)

"In the same way," my Lord said, "Moses was sent to a nation as My spokesman, and He did set his brothers free from their enslavement. It was not by his eloquence, nor by his degrees that it happened, but it was by My Spirit. In these last days, I will send many forth with My messages. As My words are obediently proclaimed, My Spirit will act. Souls will repent and turn fully to Me. All I need are those who will say yes, in faith, and who will go to those I send them."

He concluded with this clear directive for success: "Before each is called and sent, all I call must come to Me and be empowered by My Spirit. Once you are filled and immersed in My glory, I will immediately use you to gather in the harvest." (See Luke 24; 49, 53.)

Slaves to Sin

In a vision, I saw many of the people in the USA walking in slavery. Their masters controlled them here on the Earth and were slyly leading them to Hell. Shackles of anger, lust, fear, hatred, bitterness and materialism were but a few of those chains I observed wrapping around their victims. None were free and truly happy.

The few who served the Lord, totally and completely, didn't walk; they soared above all the oppression in the land and were filled with joy, peace and love. Freedom was theirs. The most troubling part of this vision was that the same freedom was offered to all, but few partook of it. Sin enslaved those who refused the Lord's invitation.

The Lord explained: "As I sent Moses to Egypt to set My children free, I send My chosen ones to those held in slavery to sin, to speak My words that bring freedom and life. Speak freely, forcefully, and with abounding love and faith. You will see those held in captivity set free. Do not withhold My words for fear of man's response but trust Me to give you the right words at the right time. Speak, and the truth will set the captives free."

Eyes Will be Opened

"The time has come for Me to act!" Jesus exclaimed. "Actions speak louder than words. Those who have remained steadfast and faithful to Me will receive their great reward. Success will follow their actions. For those who have gone their own way and refused to follow My ways, there will be a great reaping of sorrow and suffering. Truly the wages of sin are death. Those who have embraced a sinful lifestyle will begin to reap judgment in this hour. Lack will just be one of the results of their transgressions. Evil deeds will be exposed. The truth will no longer be hidden, nor will lies be accepted as truth.

"Justice demands action in this hour," He stated firmly. "For the sake of My faithful ones, I must act. Selfishness and pride will no longer be accepted or admired by the masses. Instead, humility and sacrifice will be exposed and emulated. Sin will be seen for what it is, and it will be rejected. The sham that has covered sinful actions has been lifted. Now eyes will be opened, and evil will appear as what it is. Its appeal will be lost forever. Now goodness and mercy will be glamorized. Watch as I change the tenure of the times, just by My word and by My glory!"

Lessons Learned from Jonah's Story

Scripture relates the impressive story of Jonah, a prophet of God. He was a man called by God to bring a message of repentance to a wicked city. The city God asked Jonah to go to was Nineveh, a city Jonah hated intensely. Jonah was a patriot and loved his country. Nineveh was Israel's worst enemy and had frequently attacked and pillaged its people. Instead of going to Nineveh, Jonah disobeyed

God and ran in the other direction. He boarded a ship heading for Tarshish.

As determined as Jonah was not to deliver this message, God was more determined that Jonah would, for there was a lot at stake. The people of Nineveh were God's children and would be destroyed if they did not repent. Jonah was their only hope.

Soon after boarding the ship, Jonah found a place to rest and fell into a deep sleep. God sent a mighty wind to blow upon the sea. In desperation, the sailors lightened the ship by throwing their cargo overboard. Eventually they awakened Jonah and found out that he was the reason for the storm. He was running from his God, the creator of Heaven and Earth. Filled with fear, but with no other choice, they threw Jonah into the sea. Death was awaiting Jonah.

But God had other plans; Nineveh needed to hear the word of God. God sent a large fish to swallow Jonah. While in the belly of this fish, wrapped in seaweed, Jonah came to his senses. He cried out to God and promised to serve and obey him.

Because he believed that God would help him, Jonah desperately prayed for help. True to His nature, God responded to His contrite prophet's prayers of faith and commanded the fish to spit Jonah out on the shore. Reluctantly, but in obedience, Jonah went to Nineveh and spoke God's word. He warned the people to turn from their sins, or they would be destroyed. The people of Nineveh believed; they repented and were blessed instead of destroyed. (See Jonah 2:1–10, 3; Jeremiah 18.)

As I sat before the Lord listening, He revealed a truth about the story of Jonah that I had never perceived:

"The only thing that can stop Me is unbelief. That is why the enemy works so hard to bring discouragement and fear to My children. Wrapped in the seaweed of despair, many do not cry out in faith. To cry out in faith, despite the evidence of certain destruction and failure, is faith in action. Cry out to Me, no matter how bad things appear, and I will act on your behalf. Cry out, knowing who I am and that I will act. Even those who cried out for My help, whose faith was found lacking, received their miracles.

"Without a small amount of faith, there will be no crying out for help. In order for Me to act, all that is necessary is faith the size of a mustard seed. Ask and you will receive. Seek and you will find, for I am a good God. That small faith, when it sees the results of your God acting on your behalf, will grow like the plant a mustard seed produces. Ask, and watch Me respond. Then you will see your faith and boldness grow, but first you must take the step of faith and ask!

"Trust Me, even when the wind howls and the waves of adversity rise all about you. Cry out to Me like Jonah and believe that I will act on your behalf. Believe that I will answer and that I will rescue you, and then watch as your God acts on your behalf and uses you to rescue the lost."

Fight with Faith

Once again, the Lord took me in the spirit over the USA and spoke about the great power of faith. As I looked down, I beheld misery of every kind portrayed in region after region: sickness, poverty, violence and addictions destroying people's lives.

My Friend explained the meaning of this troubling vision:

"I show you this because it is unnecessary! I defeated the devil and overcame his works. But My people insist on believing in his power, instead of putting their faith in Me. I am more powerful than poverty, blindness, deafness, illness, death, sin and addictions. Repeatedly My Word displays My power over satan, as I healed and delivered the multitudes. By the magnitude and multitude of the miracles I performed, I demonstrated My power so all would believe. It is not necessary that men suffer as they do. They have placed their faith in the power of evil, instead of in My power. Cancer, poverty and weather disasters could all be overcome by simply trusting Me to respond and by exercising the authority I have extended to My people.

"Will problems come? Yes. Will the enemy continued to throw grenades and bombs at My people? Yes, but I have overcome him. Use faith and righteousness as your shield. Remain hidden in Me. Pray with faith. Give Me those troubling issues immediately. Maintain your peace and watch Me display My power. Leave the grenades of the enemy for Me to take care of, as you pray and stay focused on Me. Then they won't blow up in your face; they will explode back into the camp of the enemy.

"Just imagine what life could be like if all would believe in what I want to do. Then My will would be done on Earth as it is in Heaven. There would be no sickness, no sorrow and no poverty. Joy unspeakable would fill every heart. The more faith is exercised, the more the Earth will resemble Heaven. My plans are to do you good, not evil. Believe it, and watch the glory of your God appear." (See 1 John 5:14.)

"Now open your spiritual eyes and see the Earth if men would believe in My power over evil. Sickness would disappear. Poverty would be overcome. Addictions would no longer destroy lives. Joy would fill the Earth. Sorrow would be destroyed.

"It's coming; the day and the hour are at hand when I will pour out My Spirit on all flesh. My Spirit will give men faith to overcome and live victorious lives. The day is at hand for My glory to be revealed. Only believe!"

As we trust and believe in Him, He will fight for us; He will hide us in the shadow of His hand. He will fulfill His promise to pour His glory out on all flesh.

> *"For I know the plans I have for you," declares the Lord, "plans to prosper you and not to harm you, plans to give you hope and a future"* (Jeremiah 29:11).

Chapter Eighteen

His Glory Is Coming to the Earth

Arise, shine, for your light has come, and the glory of the Lord rises upon you. See, darkness covers the earth and thick darkness is over the peoples, but the Lord rises upon you and his glory appears over you.

—Isaiah 60:1-2

While sitting on the garden swing in the garden of glory between Father and my Lord, Father told me:

"When you share the wonders that We have shown you, it will help My children to become much more heavenly minded. The things of the Earth will grow strangely dim. The death of loved ones, who lived their lives for Me, shall be celebrated and no longer mourned.

"Don't hold anything back but speak of the wonders of Heaven freely. All that you hear Us say, We shall bring to your remembrance, so do not be afraid you will forget anything; it is all within you."

Then, with childlike enthusiasm I beheld, the large, beautiful White Eagle, who represented Holy Spirit, appear before us. I had previously seen Him in many other visits to Heaven. "Come, I have much to show you," He said, as I left my seat between Father and Jesus. Though I could not see their faces, I did see smiles of approval, as I climbed on the back of White Eagle.

Hugging Him closely, Holy Spirit reiterated what Father told me:

"Do not be afraid to reveal all you see, all you hear and all you know about Us. Tell all of the great love Father has for His children, and tell them of the beautiful, magnificent land He has prepared for all of them. You have been given a glimpse of a few places in Heaven, but there is so much more. Larger than Earth is Heaven. Remember, it is the home of God, who creates all to reflect His goodness. His home is the biggest and best of all that He created! His heart is that none are exempt from coming to live with Him in His home. That is why He sent Jesus to the Earth—to make the way not only possible, but easy for all."

I asked Holy Spirit if He was taking me back into the natural realm, if my visit in the spirit to Heaven was over. He explained, "No, not yet. I am going to give you an aerial view of Father's kingdom today."

An Aerial Tour of Heaven

From the Mountain of Glory, we flew past the amusement park Father made for His children to enjoy, over the gardens and wheat fields, to the snowcapped mountains that glistened like they were covered with diamonds.

Holding on tightly to my Friend, He flew over a vast land. I was privileged to hear laughter and joyful singing and music flowing into the air. There was no sadness, no fighting, no riots and no disagreements in any region we flew over—just joy, love and great peace filled the atmosphere that covered this land. I thought, "This is so different than where I live on the Earth. Here we have heated arguments, violence, sadness, strife and even riots."

Knowing my thoughts, Holy Spirit explained, "This is why Father is going to pour His glory out on the Earth. The Earth was made to reflect the glory of Heaven, but it has been overtaken by evil forces. To return the whole Earth—not just your nation—to its original design, can only happenif Father pours forth on the land below some of what Heaven holds. Light causes darkness to flee. Good shall overcome evil, as Father pours His goodness out on all flesh."

Alone flying with the Holy Spirit, Father spoke these comforting words to my heart:

"I have heard the cries of My people, and I will pour My glory forth, so that what you see, feel and hear in Heaven, you will see, feel and hear on Earth, too. I created man in My image—to be like Me—full of love, goodness and strength. My will shall be done on Earth as it is in Heaven! There is no worry, hatred or fear in Heaven, and My love poured out on your land will cause fear to flee, hatred to be destroyed and love to flow."

He promised me: "Those who read and hear you speak of what you experienced here in Heaven—your homeland—will feel the same love, peace and joy that you feel as you encounter Us."

The King of Glory Lives in You

Days later, and once again alone in the spirit with Jesus, my wonderful Friend gave me a message to deliver to His loved ones:

"Tell My people that the King of Glory dwells within them. In truth, the Kingdom of God is within them, but they must allow Me to reign on the throne of their heart. Many of them have idols, or even have themselves, sitting on the throne inside them; I am ignored. Unless a King is allowed to rule, he cannot exercise his full authority. I want to reign in My children's lives so I can rescue them from every tyrant that comes against them. But if they don't acknowledge Me as their King, My hands are tied.

"Friendship with the King is the relationship I have called all My children to, but few, so very few, have answered the call to be My true friend. Friends walk and talk together. They seek to help one another and love to bless each other. I want to say to each one, 'You are my friend.' But I can't, because I only speak what is true.

"While reading Scripture, how many people did I call friends of God? Of the thousands and thousands mentioned in My Word, only a handful were called My friends. Those who were My friend stood out among the rest. They ruled in their neighborhood, because I ruled through them. They spoke and others listened, because I spoke through them. They walked and their shadows healed the sick, because My shadow covered them. My glory poured out of them!

"I want to say to My people, 'Eat and be satisfied; partake of Me who dwells within you and you will never be hungry again.'

"There will be no more thirsting after what will not satisfy once they have found Me as their Friend and King. Again, the things of the world will grow strangely dim as the glory of My Kingdom is revealed to them. All vain seeking will end once I am found. Taste and see how good the Lord is. This is My invitation to My people: come and experience My glory, and you will find My love to be all sufficient."

Lessons learned about Father's Glory

For the Lord has redeemed Jacob, he displays his glory in Israel (Isaiah 44:23).

Back in the spirit one quiet morning, I saw myself lying on the beach in Heaven beside Jesus. Looking up, I saw the golden sky above. From this shimmering sky, liquid gold poured forth all over the land and sea—and on us.

Holding my hand in His, Jesus said, "As you cannot stop the rain from falling on the Earth, no one will stop Us from pouring Our glory forth on all mankind. No one can stop what We declare—no one! Glory will fall and the darkness will flee.

"Those who are Our vessels, that We have cloaked in Our glory, will shine brightly for all to see. Our glory pouring off Our beloved ones will scatter the darkness in Our children's lives. As each one soaks in the spirit, with Our glory pouring forth on them, because they are being thoroughly saturated in Our glory, they will easily be a vessel We use to pour Our glory out of, to those steeped in darkness.

"In the past, I showed you how easy it would be to bring in the harvest by just lying beside us in intimate fellowship; just as easy will it be for My faithful ones to display Our great glory. The enemy has attempted to spread his deadly plague of Covid-19 through contagion; now I will use contagion to spread My glory. Those permeated with My glory will be used to spread Our love, Our presence, Our healing, Our miracles, Our words and Our works for all to see and to receive.

"Just soaking in Our glory is all My children need to do to be equipped! The more time they spend soaking in Our goodness and Our glory, the more of Our glory and Our goodness they will receive. Encourage My friends to be great glory soakers! As they listen and obey, they will see wonderful miracles take place so easily, it will amaze them!

"Glory will be their portion and the portion of this world. In this hour, My glory will overtake the gross darkness of this world. Evil will be exposed for what it is and so will My goodness, as it manifests through My people who are saturated and soaked in My glory. Let My light shine through you for all to see. Never be ashamed of My glory."

Encouraged to Seek His Glory Daily

Jesus continued teaching me about His glory: "Stay soaking daily in My glory, and let My glory invade your land, as it pours off you. Reach out and touch the hungry ones I send to you, and My glory will touch them. After My glory is received, each one will be changed quickly. The more My glory is manifested, the more of My miracles will happen."

He declared, "Keep pressing in to receive much more of My glory, then all things will be made easy. Watch, as My glory makes all We give you to do happen with very little effort on your part. The solution to all problems is My glory. As My tangible presence, My goodness, My Spirit invade you and your land, the terrible problems that seem impossible to fix will be changed. Yes, rejoicing will replace sorrow; joy will overtake depression; faith will chase fear away; My peace will make all unrest and turmoil—and rioting—leave! My glory is the answer. As My children cry out for My glory, miracles will happen worldwide."

His Glory Will Bring Unity

One day, to my great pleasure, the Lord brought me to one of my favorite places in Heaven, the Hall of Miracles. Unbeknownst to me, He was going to show me another wonderful fruit of the outpouring of His glory. As we walked together into the entrance to the golden hall, My wonderful Father greeted me.

He was waiting for my arrival: "Daughter, in the past your curiosity and excitement lead you to the rooms on the left side of this hall. Today I want to show you what you missed on the right side of the hall."

Before Father showed me the room I missed seeing on the left side of this glorious hall, He brought me to the large warehouse room on the right side of the hall. Previously, it was filled to the brim with houses, cars, motorcycles, bikes, clothes, furniture, etc. but today the room was not so full.

He explained: "My children are beginning to seek My face, pray, and turn from their sins, so I am able to send them many wonders from Heaven. When Holy Spirit is poured out on all flesh, these rooms will all be empty and just filled with the sounds of rejoicing and great glory. Now come see what I long to show you."

With His loving arm about my shoulder, and Jesus beside me holding my hand in His, we walked together toward the special room. Approaching the doorway, I knew this room was special to my Father; it depicted what was coming to the Earth in the future. Wonderful miracles are held here in each room on the Hall of Miracles, awaiting the Father's children, when they humble themselves, pray, seek His face and turn from their wicked ways.

To my astonishment as we walked in the room, I saw families laughing and enjoying one another's company. They were sitting at tables eating, laughing and talking together.

"This is coming, my friend. Harmony will once again pour forth from this room called 'unity' to My children. So many suffer alone, wounded and ostracized by their families, but that will change when Holy Spirit brings the unity from Heaven to Earth. Families will be restored and reunited; it will happen very quickly for My Spirit is adept at doing a quick work in the hearts of My children. Continue to pray for the great outpouring of My Spirit, for I long to see the unity that fills Heaven flood the Earth." As I heard my Father say all this, I heard deep belly laughter resounding through this room.

I knew the reason that there was such happiness and unity that was imparted and flourishing in this room: everyone here had received the gift of being able to see what Father sees in each one. All the goodness He had put in every person was visible to all and being celebrated. There was no jealousy or competition in this room, the contents of which would soon be sent to the Earth.

The outpouring of His great glory will bring abundant restoration to families! As I watched this delightful scene, I received the understanding that Holy Spirit is even going to unite families that were separated because of mental illness and addictions. The homeless and rejected ones would be delivered and healed in this revival; they would be accepted back in their families. What glory awaits us all! It was time for me to go, but I knew that in the days ahead my Lord and my Father would bring me back to see what lay behind many of the other doors on the right side of the Hall of Miracles.

His Glory is the Answer

After watching the news, great concern had filled my being over the state of our nation. With love and compassion He spoke words that brought peace to my storm-tossed heart:

"The fear of the Lord shall be pouring out on your land in this hour. Knees will bow before Us; sincere commitments shall be made to Us. Yes, the fear of the Lord is the beginning of wisdom.

"Many foolish decisions have been made by My children, because they lack a true fear of Me. My ways are not embraced, so there is no wisdom. This will change. In this hour, the masses will turn back to Me and embrace My ways as their own.

"I am deeply concerned over the state of My children's hearts. They are steeped in wickedness; goodness is found in few. Their hearts are far from Us. They long for the things of this world and few long for Us. They are captured by wickedness; deception rules over their minds. I don't! My ways are shunned and spoken of with disdain. Few worship the God who created and sustains them.

"This is why we must pour Holy Spirit out on your land. Only My goodness will change this world. Elections won't; great leaders don't, but I will!

"My love turned Saul into and ambassador of truth and love. His murderous, judgmental heart was changed by one encounter with Me. I am the answer to your nation. No matter who is put in position to lead your land, they cannot change the wicked into holy men and women, but I can!" (See Acts 9.)

"Yes, pray for good leaders. Pray for My will to be done in your government but pray harder for My spirit to be poured out on your land. That will bring about lasting change and transformed lives.

"Elections won't change lives, but I will! Wicked rulers led the nation of Israel, but I still poured out My spirit and did transform multitudes in spite of those wicked kings and their officials. I am bigger than the wickedness of governments and news media outlets. I am the hope of your nation. When I come, I bring love, joy, peace, patience, kindness, goodness, faithfulness, gentleness and self-control. Even great leaders cannot do this!" (See Galatians 5:22.)

"Yes, it is My will for you to have godly government. By My Spirit this will happen, and by My Spirit the masses will turn from wickedness to righteousness. Goodness will be emulated and evil seen for what it is and rejected.

"Fire from Heaven will fall on all, both the good and the evil. The chaff of wickedness will be consumed. A holy hunger for love and truth will be instilled in all. The battle for righteousness will no longer be so fierce, because most will shun evil and embrace My goodness. This will happen in your world and in the prisons which hold many who are possessed by wickedness. They, too, shall be set free.

"Once My Spirit falls on all, no longer will evil appeal to My children. A true hunger for righteousness will be embraced and a rejection of evil, vain philosophies will prevail in your land—and in others, too."

> *Then the Lord spoke to Job..."Do you have an arm like God's, and can your voice thundered like his? Unleash the fury of your wrath, look at every proud man and bring him low, look at every proud man and humble him, crush the wicked where they stand. Then I myself will admit to you that your own right hand can save you"* (Job 40:6, 9, 11, 12, 14).

Only God could save Job from his suffering. His own strength couldn't do it, nor can our own strength or the strength of any man save us. Only God!

Chapter Nineteen

We Will See His Glory

For the earth will be filled with the knowledge of the glory of the Lord, as the waters cover the sea.
—Habakkuk 2:14

After hearing my Lord promise that He would be pouring out His glory all over the world, and knowing well that His great glory is our only hope; I sought His help. Understanding well my desperation for the outpouring of His glory, He encouraged my faith with these words:

"As the worshipers arise, I will respond with an outpouring of My glory. My glory will chase evil away. Yes, all that is birthed by evil will have to leave. In My presence is the fullness of joy. Nothing that diminishes joy will be allowed to stay when My glory arrives! Just have faith in Me and in My truths that I show you, and you will see My glory, and all the effects of it, on your land.

"Light always disperses the darkness and My glory is light; it will disperse the darkness that has overtaken your land. Those who love the darkness will see darkness for what it is and hate it. They will run to the light and leave what hides in the darkness. Those who have created the darkness will no longer be able to deceive the masses into thinking that good is evil and that evil is good. My light will shine truth forth. Once My children are touched by the truth, they will never be the same. No longer will they believe lies, but will reject the liars who have deceived them. A great turning is coming on your world, for the glory is coming!"

His Glory Clearly Explained

With great clarity, Father explained: "You cannot separate My glory from Me or from who I am. My glory is My essence, My fragrance, My nature and My being. Just as your humanity cannot be separated from you—that is who you are—human; in the same way, My glory cannot be separated from Me. Wherever I am, that is where My glory is."

Then He gave me a wonderful promise for the future: "The days ahead will be marked by My glory. Being flooded with My glory will become commonplace and expected by all. A new addiction will overtake My children—an avarice addiction to My glory! In the days ahead, you will see many transformed from Saul, the persecutor of My people, to Paul, the apostle to the Gentiles. Many will leave their ignorance and embrace the wisdom, knowledge and glory of My kingdom."

Trained to Sustain His Presence

A few days later while alone in my prayer room, expectation filled my heart. I could sense that today I was going to see something wonderful and hear from my faithful Friend. I was not disappointed. He always responds to faith:

"Practice makes perfect. Only those who have allowed Us to train them in the ways of the Spirit will be able to sustain the heavyweight of My great glory during the great outpouring. This is the preparation I have called My children to, but few listened.

For those few who listened and obeyed, they will be mightily used in the days ahead, for they will be able to sustain and manage My power as it pours forth on and through them," I heard Jesus say, as I saw myself in the spirit walking beside Him on the shore of the ocean.

Suddenly, a great tsunami wave appeared and fell right over the top of us. The Lord explained that the season we had been in is like the time just before a tsunami hits, when the water recedes dramatically. There has been a dearth of the Spirit. The church and its people have been walking in a time of dryness; but now there will be the great outpouring. For those who continued to seek Him in spite of the dryness, who sat with Him in fellowship, who drank deep of His presence and who practiced using the gifts of the Holy Spirit: these are ready for what is coming.

I saw the wave hit us, but Jesus and I stayed standing while all about us were knocked down and were tumbling in the water. I asked the Lord why it was important to stay standing when this wave of glory hits, and He explained that those who are trained in the Spirit are like soldiers who have been trained for combat. They are adept at using their weapons. The Lord wants us well trained to use our weapons, too: the gift of miracles, words of knowledge, prophecy, supernatural faith, words of wisdom, discerning of spirits, healing, tongues and interpretation of tongues.

To just roll around on the floor in enjoyment and to be submersed in His glory will be fun, but the Lord has asked us to prepare because with the greater glory there will be much responsibility. Souls will need to be saved, delivered, healed, taught and raised up, but only those who listened and obeyed His leadings to get ready will be able to be used so powerfully and effectively.

As we spend time daily soaking in His glory, Holy Spirit will teach us how to manage the glory, so that we can function and be effective in helping His children. There is no other way to get ready for the greater glory that is coming! A few days later, He met with me and explained that there is a price we must pay to carry His glory. That price is spending time with Him daily soaking in His glory and being groomed by Holy Spirit in His ways.

Flames of Fire

"Fires of revival are breaking out all over your land," I heard as Jesus and I sat on the bench on top of the mountain of intimacy that overlooks the world. "My children are as flames of fire. Those who sit with Us, and burn with passion for Us, will be set ablaze by My glory and will be used to ignite these fires in different regions. Only those who pay the price of sweet fellowship will be used to ignite these fires.

"I will be sending My friends forth in this land as burning ones. Like a fiery torch in the hand of their God, they will go and spread the fire of deep passion for Us. The very dry, thirsty ones will easily catch ablaze. These fires, which they light by the power of Holy Spirit, will never go out but will burn indefinitely.

"This is why My friends have been kept separate and hidden by My hand; the time was not right and My children not ready to catch this glory fire, but now is the hour. Yes, the hour is at hand for fresh fire from Heaven to fall. This fire of My glory will not only fuel passion for Me and for the lost, but it will burn the chaff in My children and cause them to be holy ones. Once they are touched by My glory fire, each one will become passionate for Us, shun evil, and deny their flesh the pleasures that once controlled them."

Expand Your Faith for the Hour Is at Hand

A few days later while in the spirit, sitting in Heaven next to my Father in His cozy den, I listened attentively as He explained:

"Suddenly you will see things happen that you have prayed and longed for, while waiting patiently for Me to act. Now I will pour out My Spirit. Now I will act on your behalf and on behalf of all those who have steadfastly loved and served Me. Suddenly My presence will be felt. Suddenly blind eyes will see and deaf ears will hear. Suddenly you will see the glory of your God manifest in tangible demonstrations.

"Not just in your church, or in your community, or in your nation, but all over this world you will see the glory of your God manifested. Prayers prayed in one region will bear fruit everywhere. What I do for one, I will do for all. I do cause the rain to fall on the just and the unjust at the same time. I will rain My power and glory down on all mankind.

"When you pray for your nation and your leaders, watch as I perform those requests in other nations and transform their leaders. An explosion of multiplication is coming in this next great move of God. As I came only to the Jewish nation and then transferred their blessings to the Gentiles, I will do the same in this hour. I will bless those near and those far away as well. I will deliver, heal and prosper the masses worldwide. Expand your faith in your requests, for I am well able to accomplish all!"

The River of God

> *The man brought me back to the entrance of the temple, and I saw the water coming out from under the threshold of the temple toward the east (for the temple faced the*

> *east). The water was coming down from under the south side of the temple, south of the altar... He measured off another thousand and led me through water that was up to the waist* (Ezekiel 47:1,4).

A few days later Father continued to promise: "For I have heard the ardent cries of My children, and now is the time for Me to act on their behalf. That is why the outpouring of My Spirit is pictured as rain. It soaks everyone. It is no respecter of persons. The heavens are heavy with My weighty glory. The storm clouds are gathering, and I will command them to release that which they have stored up in them—My Spirit to the Earth. That is why I say whole families, regions and nations will be impacted by My glory in this hour.

"None will be able to escape the good that I have for them, for I cause the sun to shine on the just and the unjust alike. My Spirit will render each one useless to the enemy and make them useful to Me overnight!

"My rain will rise up those who are dead in their trespasses and sins. Alive—they will assemble as a mighty army and advance in this land. They will conquer the foe that once held them in bondage. Where they were once weak, I will become their greatest strength."

While I listened to my Father speak, I looked into the spirit and saw His form before me. He was sitting on His throne so majestic, but also so loving and kind. As I looked and listened, I became aware that I was about chest deep in water. I was at His feet, yet I was in the river—in the river of glory! The river of life and glory that flows from His throne was the river of sweet communion and peace.

Then the angel showed me the river of the water of life, as clear as crystal, flowing from the throne of God and of the Lamb down the middle of the great street of the city (Revelation 22:1–2).

Revelation of Jesus in the River

As I sat before Him, I was given the understanding that this was the place Jesus went to 2000 years ago, when He ascended the mountain to get apart with His Father. He went into the spirit realm and sat before His Father in the river of glory—the river of peace and sweet communion. (See Luke 5:16.) Empowered by peace and love, He returned to those who needed His touch and His word. The river of life and glory flowed forth from Jesus. (See John 7:37.)

If we want to be renewed and refilled daily, so that the same river of glory that flows from the throne of God will pour out of our lives, we must sit at the feet of the Father, too.

The next morning when I entered the spirit realm, I saw the throne of God in the distance. The river of life was flowing from it. As I peered deeper into the spirit realm, I saw people coming from either side of the river. Some couldn't get to the river, because they were chained to a tree. Quietly, Jesus walked over to them and set them free. They went forth gingerly toward the river. Most knew He had set them free, while a few didn't fully realize what He had done for them. As I looked closer, I watched as a group ran toward the river because their friends were encouraging them to jump in. Many people were scattered about in all different places and at different depths in the river, but all were heading upstream where the Father and His Son waited for them.

What a sight I was privileged to observe! There is freedom in the river of glory—freedom from all bondage. Everything you need is found in the river: healing, prosperity, reconciliation and total restoration of all that has been stolen. Jesus is the only way to the river of life and glory that flows from the throne of God. Believing, following and loving Jesus will bring you in this river. As we consecrate more and more of ourselves to the Lord, we will go deeper in the river and draw closer to the Father. Breathless, I realized that the river of glory and life represented the precious Holy Spirit. He takes us to the Father and the Son, if we will just follow Him there.

Then He whispered, "When I say advance, don't be reluctant to go wherever and to whomever I lead you. Each step you take in sync with Me will lead you deeper into the river of My presence. Listen and I will lead you to the throne room, to the bosom of the Father. All you need for a full, successful life will be found there."

> *...those who are led by the Spirit of God are the sons of God* (Romans 8:14).

A Suddenly Hour

> *The hand of the Lord was upon me, and he brought me out by the spirit of the Lord and set me in the middle of a Valley; it was full of bones. He asked me, "Son of Man, can these bones live?" So I prophesied as he commanded me, and breath entered them; they came to life and stood up on their feet—a vast army* (Ezekiel 37:1, 3, 10).

One morning, as I sat listening to my Friend, He revealed His plans to me:

"Just as I prophesied through Ezekiel that I would rise up a vast army through a valley of dry bones, I say I will rise up an end-time army with My glory from the dry and desolate ones (see Ezekiel 37:1-14). Those who feel they have nothing to give; I will anoint and appoint to do great feats in My name. The most common, the most ordinary and untalented, I will use. Those who are forlorn, desperate, and afraid of failing, I will equip to be very successful.

"And they will never forget where they came from. They will remember that I walked past them and saw them just as hopeless and as desperate as a dead body left to deteriorate in an open field. I have seen their ruined lives, and I will resurrect them. They will never forget from whence I took them. Each one will know that it was I that took them by the hand, loved them, and led them on the path of success.

"Hold fast to this word, this promise, for you will see it fulfilled. Not only will you see resurrected lives, but you will see appreciation and eternal gratitude lifted to Me."

With a serious tone, He reminded me that His glory would be revealed suddenly:

"For what I will do—I will do suddenly. Like a storm on a summer afternoon, I will appear in My children's lives and suddenly shower My help upon them. Marriages will be restored, bondages to sin broken, bodies and minds healed, ministries birthed and promoted in an instant. You will see this in the lives of others and in your own life as well!

"Suddenly I rose from the dead. Suddenly the stone was rolled back, and I came forth. Suddenly those long dead and buried rose and walked the earth. Suddenly blind eyes opened and saw. Deaf ears heard. Dull minds understood. Death was conquered and life, resurrection life, was released to My people by My glory.

"Suddenly I came to the Earth, though long prophesied. In this hour, those things long promised and prophesied will be fulfilled. It will happen suddenly so all will know that no man, no institution did it. They will give the honor and praise where it is due.

"My friend, you are living in a suddenly hour, just like the world did 2000 years ago. Suddenly salvation came, death was destroyed, satan defeated, and God and man were reunited!

"Innate in the word 'suddenly' is the word 'unexpectedly.' When My children least expect it, I will come and act! Just keep your eyes and attention fixed on Me, and suddenly I will act on your behalf when you least expect it."

He ended this encounter by reminding me what happened Easter morning: "Sunday morning while all slept, weary with fear and discouragement, locked away from those they knew would kill them, My disciples trembled. At the same time, the earth trembled as My power and My glory appeared; My grave clothes were discarded. Suddenly fear, exhaustion, and depression were replaced by joy, courage, and life—a life of vision, hope and success. The same is going to happen in this hour suddenly!" (See Zechariah 10:6–12; Matthew 4:15–25; Daniel 9:4–19.)

A Call to Celebrate

> *What I tell you in the dark, speak in the day light; what is whispered in your ear, proclaim from the roofs* (Matthew 10:27).

My Lord came to me with good news: "Glory will fill your land! All that we have spoken to you shall come to pass quickly!

A mighty wind will blow through your land, and it will scatter the enemy. The breath of God, My Spirit, shall blow like a mighty wind, and the dust of evil shall be exposed and blown away. Goodness will remain and evil will be shunned; evil will no longer be accepted as good.

"The counterfeits to righteousness will be seen for what they are and will be soundly rejected. Those who were duped into thinking that evil was good and good was evil will have the blinders stripped off their eyes when My wind blows through the land. There will be a mass exodus from the camp of the enemy. Like the prodigal son did run from evil into the arms of his father, My wayward children shall run into My outstretched arms. There will be great celebrations that are attended by the masses!

"You will see victory and My glory pouring forth on your land and many others. My light, My love and My glory will shine forth through all who are laying down a sacrifice of prayer, fasting and worship for your nation. Much good will come forth; We have many who allow themselves to be used by Us to house Our glory. You will see Us work out for good all the enemy attempted to do to harm you and your nation.

"I do have a mighty army of humble ones that is partnering with Us and our angels. Their prayers of faith and their acts of love and sacrifice will bear the fruit of peace, love, unity and righteousness. I will use for good the evil that has been launched against your nation, by causing people to see evil for what it is. They will reject that evil and those used by the foe to promote it as good."

> *There is nothing concealed that will not be disclosed, or hidden that will not be made known* (Matthew 10:26).

Chapter Twenty

He Will Use the Lowly to Confound the Wise

And a little child will lead them.

—Isaiah 11:6

Filled with expectancy and great joy, I saw myself clothed in the beautiful, white, jeweled dress that I often have on when I visit my Lord in Heaven. This day, while in the spirit, I was sitting on the bench beside Jesus, where we often sit together observing what is happening on the Earth. Looking intently through Jesus, I saw young children searching for the true meaning of life.

Brokenhearted, because these highly valued little ones are so precious to Him, He said: "These are My precious gems. I treasure them more than the gold and diamonds men value on the Earth. When I look upon them My heart breaks, for many are neglected and others misled by those I have placed in their lives to guide them into truth. These sad little children are being left to their own devices and have to figure out for themselves what the true meaning of life is.

"But, My daughter," He began to explain His plan for the future of these little ones; "I am not leaving them or forsaking these so beloved by Me. I have dispatched My angels to attend them. They have received their assignment to bring the truth to each one. Many young ones will be seeing visions, hearing inspired messages, and dreaming dreams of heavenly places. In the coming days, there will be reports of these events reaching the ears of the adults who need these truths, and they will be dramatically inspired by them."

Then I heard the Father interject: "No matter what others tell them or what the media presents to their youthful minds, they won't continue to be misled, because they have experienced the truth. They will spot a cheap imitation of the truth because they have known the valuable revelation of My Son. These young ones will not be satisfied with the cheap baubles of fantasy the enemy is using to deceive them. Witchcraft will not interest them, because I do. My little ones will fall in love with My Son and teach others of His great love for them."

Children Will Rule on His Behalf

Jesus explained further: "Young ones with the same character as David, Samuel, Esther, Mary and John the Baptist are once again being groomed by Me for the great final outpouring of My glory. And a little child shall lead them (see Isaiah 11:6). The wisdom these chosen little ones will possess will not be refuted by even the most astute. I will take them from all sectors of society and many nations and give them a special seat in My kingdom.

"Yes, I say seat, for they will sit on thrones and judge many. While they are upon the Earth, they will rule with the rod of My authority. The faith of these little one will be great; they will confound many. Mountain-moving, miracle-working faith will be the earmark of these that are filled with My presence. They will display My glory for all to see, for it truly is not by power, nor by might, but by My Spirit. These children will represent this truth for all to recognize; their God could be using them to shine through." (See Zechariah 4:6.)

Amazed by what my Lord was telling me, He explained; "Once again I bring a child before My people, and I say: Unless you become like a little child, you shall not enter the kingdom of Heaven. Unless your faith surpasses the faith of the scribes and the Pharisees, you will not enter My kingdom. Let the faith of My little children be a demonstration of the faith I want in all My children." (See Matthew 18:2-6.)

Intently looking into Jesus' eyes, He asked me: "Do you see what I see? Do you see the great sorrow and emptiness that fills many of these little ones? Because My life does not fill the lives of their caretakers, My love is not being displayed to them. A great void fills their lives. Wherever there is a void, the enemy attempts to fill it with his lies. Where love is not displayed, hatred and abuse are depicted. Indifference engulfs the hearts that yearn for attention and concern."

As I looked upon these children in this vision, I saw the great emptiness that consumed many of these little ones motivate them to seek inappropriate activities to comfort and occupy themselves.

Then I heard, "Every void must be filled, every valley filled, every crooked path made straight, for the kingdom of God is coming."

He will come and fill them with His love! What a wonderful plan the Lord has set in place to rescue His precious children and to use them in the coming revival. His glory will shine upon them and pour out of them to the world. And their joy will be complete in Him. The future is bright for those who decide to live for Him.

> *A voice of one calling: "In the desert prepare the way for the Lord; make straight in the wilderness a highway for our God. Every valley shall be raised up, every mountain and hill made low; the rough ground shall become level, the rugged places a plain. And the glory of the Lord will be revealed, and all mankind together will see it. For the mouth of the Lord has spoken"* (Isaiah 40:3-5).

He Will Turn Our Sorrows into Joys

> *The poor and needy search for water; but there is none; their tongues are parched with thirst. But I the Lord will answer them; I, the God of Israel, will not forsake them. I will make rivers flow on barren heights and springs within the valleys. I will turn the desert into pools of water, and the parched ground into springs* (Isaiah 41:17-18).

The Lord never ceases to amaze and surprise me. He appeared to me in a vision and invited me to go for a ride to the heights with Him on the glorious, white eagle. As in the past, I climbed upon my friend, the great, white eagle, and flew far away beside Jesus.

This enormous bird took me to the rock seat on the top of the mountain where Jesus watches over the Earth. Sitting down next to my Lord, He explained that today He was going to take me to the bowels of the Earth. While I listened to Jesus, a donkey appeared for each of us to ride upon. Without any further explanation, we climbed upon the donkeys and descended down a steep grade to a lowly place.

He Will Ride Upon a Donkey Once Again

After riding in silence for a while Jesus spoke:

"This is where the poor and the desperate ones live, My child. Those in need of food, clothing and health live here. In the past, I rode on a donkey within Mary's womb to rescue mankind from their hard taskmaster. Thirty-three years later, again I rode upon a donkey into Jerusalem to rescue My people from the snare of sin. Now is the hour when I shall again mount upon a donkey and descend to the Earth for a final attempt to rescue all who have not found life."

I realized He was not talking about His second coming, but He was talking about the next great move of God. Before He comes on His white horse, as He has promised, He will first come through His lowly ones to bring His gifts and glory to His beloved ones. He will pour His Spirit out on all flesh!

Interrupting my thoughts He said: "Those dead in sin live within the bowels of the Earth. They might dwell in palatial homes by the seashore, but truly, they are without life. They dwell in the place of the desperate and the dead. I am sending you to the bowels of the Earth to rescue those who have never tasted My life-giving presence. Just as in the past, I rode upon a donkey, not a mighty white stallion; once again I will ride, through My bride, upon the lowly ones, those considered to be like a donkey in the eyes of men."

> *Brothers, think of what you were when you were called. Not many of you were wise by human standards; not*

> *many were influential; not many were of noble birth. But God chose the foolish things of the world to shame the wise; God chose the weak things of the world to shame the strong. He chose the lowly things of this world and the despised things—and the things that are not—to nullify the things that are, so that no one may boast before him* (1 Corinthians 1:26-29).

With great compassion in His voice, He spoke about the future: "The lowly will inherit the Earth, and the proud will be turned away. Come, meek and lowly; come with Me to rescue the living dead who dwell in darkness and despair. Fear enshrouds them, because they have no deliverer.

"I am the same yesterday, today and forever. Forever I am lowly and meek, but valiant. That is who you follow and serve. It is the meek and the lowly that will inherit the Earth. The proud will be turned aside. Follow Me meekly to the bowels of the Earth and let Me use you to pull them out of the darkness and the place of lack where they dwell, into the high places of victory and everlasting joy forever.

"Only those riding on a lowly donkey will be permitted to rescue My children. The high and the mighty ones are not following Me and will not descend to the bowels of the Earth as rescuers. They have lost their way and must return to Me to find the route I take to deliver and rescue the lifeless. My ways are not your ways, nor are My thoughts yours when you seek to serve Me in splendor and ease.

"Remember I am the deliverer who arrived on a lowly donkey. That is who you follow and serve. Any other will not be recognized, nor will they be successful, because I am not leading them.

The path I take is not a glamorous, comfortable way, and few find it. Only those who ride upon the wings of My Spirit find the way to touch the hearts of the dead and bring life. It is only through Me, with Me, and in Me that any good will be accomplished. All else will burn away as chaff. Remember it is the lowly who will inherit the Earth, not those who are high and mighty in their own estimation. If I, the King of Glory, could ride upon a donkey to rescue the world, why shouldn't My followers do the same? It is only by taking the low road that the heights will be reached."

During this dramatic encounter, I grew to understand the heart of my Friend toward His bride. He is going to choose those in the church who don't have an exalted opinion of themselves or their ministries to gather in the lost. He made it clear that only those who are tenderhearted and humble will be sent to rescue His people.

I also became aware that because of His tender mercies, God the Father is giving the world time to receive His Son's free gift of salvation offered through the helping hands of His humble servants.

Though He expressed His heart using the prophetic picture of riding through His friends on a humble donkey, I know that the time is short and the day fast approaching when Jesus will appear, not riding on a donkey, or coming through His humble bride to seek the lost, but He will come in all of His majesty and power, riding on His white horse to judge all mankind and to rule the Earth.

> *I saw heaven standing open and there before me was a white horse, whose rider is called Faithful and True. With justice he judges and makes war. His eyes are like blazing fire, and on his head are many crowns. ...his*

name is the word of God. The armies of heaven were following him, riding on white horses and dressed in fine linen, white and clean. On his robe and on his thigh he has this name written: King of Kings and Lord of Lords (Revelation 19:11–12,14,16).

Believe in the God Who Made Everything Out of Nothing

He made the earth by his power; he founded the world by his wisdom and stretched out the heavens by his understanding. When he thunders, the waters in the heavens roar; he made clouds rise from the ends of the earth. He sends lightening with the rain and brings out the wind from his storehouses (Jeremiah 51:15-16).

While contemplating God's incredible plan to use children and those that the world disregards in the end-time revival, I heard the familiar voice of my Lord: "Today, I would have you look at My creation."

With incredible speed, Jesus took me in the spirit, throughout the world, to view all that He had made. Vast oceans, snow covered mountains, valleys and lakes, the sun high in the sky, the moon and the stars shining against the dark night sky, lush green grass, birds and animals flying and scampering about the fields, tall cedar trees, pine trees of all shapes and sizes, fruit trees, every tree you could imagine, babbling brooks, the majestic Grand Canyon: all passed before my sight.

Believe and You Will See

Then my Friend explained: "All that I have shown you was created out of nothing. The sun did not exist before I did, but I spoke it into existence. I spoke and 'nothing' took form and became something exquisite.

"Give Me your nothingness," He declared. "Give Me your loaves and fish, and watch what I do with them. Give Me your inabilities and weaknesses and watch as I speak to them. Watch the stutter and the stammered speak, as I declare it to be so. Many times My people see weakness and their own deficiencies and are stopped short. If they would look and see the God who created all out of nothing; if they would look and see the God who fed the multitudes with the handful of loaves and fish; if they would look and see the God who used Moses, who stutter and stammered, to release a nation from captivity; they would see their own deliverance."

Increasing my faith in His ability to use the lowly to rescue the oppressed, Jesus said, "I still speak. I still create something out of nothing, if I am given the opportunity. As you surrender your nothingness, I will speak to it, and, out of nothing, you will see something appear. You will see the fearful and the timid courageously perform miracles in My name. You will see the lame leap. The secret to success is to humbly submit your weaknesses to Me, because you know who I am, and out of nothing I create something.

"Let your faith arise in the God who cares for you. Because I love you, I will turn your sorrows into joy. I will make the impossible happen easily by My spoken word. Simply believe, and watch as the God who cares for you undertake all that concerns you. Stand fast when trouble or challenges comes your way, and remember the God who made everything out of nothing."

> *In the beginning was the Word, and the Word was with God, and the Word was God. He was with God in the beginning. Through him all things were made; without him nothing was made that has been made* (John 1:1-3).

Chapter Twenty-One

JUSTICE WILL BRING CHANGE!

Righteousness and justice are the foundation of your throne; love and faithfulness go before you.

—PSALM 89:14

In many impacting encounters, my Lord showed me the heart of our Father toward those who seek His glory and seek justice. It is His deep desire that truth and justice walk together though our land and in our lives. During our times together, He promised me that Father is going to answer the cries of His children for justice.

While walking in the spirit on an ocean beach with Jesus, I was shocked at what appeared before us. As we walked and talked together, I thought of some of our other trips to the beach together and wondered if I would see some of the things I had encountered on our previous visits here. In the past I saw a gentle dolphin named Grace, the ocean liner, Trust, and another day I just relaxed beside Jesus under the rainbow sky and soaked in Father's glory. This was not what I encountered! High above us, and completely encompassing the shore ahead, was a monstrous ocean wave, which was frozen in time.

Jesus explained: "This is what is coming to your world and to your life. When it is released and does hit, all it touches will never be the same."

Listening to Jesus and drawing very close to Him, while holding His hand, we walked under this massive, dark wave. It was so enormous and thick, no light could penetrate it. Darkness enveloped us and, as we advanced, it became a large canopy hanging in the air over us.

He explained: "Very soon this wave will appear for all to see and encounter. Encourage My children to stay close to Me, while the changes this wave brings falls upon them. You have been asking Me why I haven't shown you what is coming. Today I am opening your eyes to see this massive wave called, 'Change'! Some will embrace this change, as it will bring some people many blessings, while others will have their world destroyed by its impact.

"'Change' will be bringing justice and judgment when it arrives. Those who have walked in obedient fellowship with Us will only experience great good, when 'Change' arrives. For those who denied Us, walked away from Our ways and followed the ways of the evil one, 'Change' will turn their world upside down.

"Things that were hidden before 'Change' hits will be exposed for all to see. Shame will displace pride and arrogance. Ill-gotten wealth will disappear and poverty will remain. The acceptance of those they deceived shall come tumbling down, and they will only see the backs of those who leave them in disgust.

"A great wave of change is being released now. It will disrupt the common place, and bring turmoil to the land; but for the sake of justice, 'Change' must be sent forth. This change is being sent in answer to the cries of My children for true justice. It will not just impact the noteworthy, but all inhabitants of the land will know 'Change.'

"All who listened to the warnings to draw close to Us and to turn in sincere repentance from their sins will experience great, wonderful transformation—even My glory! Those who heard the cry to prepare for what is coming by truly getting to know Me and refused, will wish they had listened, because the change that comes upon them will not be welcomed or considered good."

Change Will Be Long Lasting

While I walked beside Jesus under this massive, dark wave, I felt protected and great peace filled my being. I was not afraid, because I knew I would be safe and live blessed. Because of the size of this wave, I realized it would encompass the world—not just my nation.

As we continued walking under this ominous covering of water, held fast in its place above us, He explained, "Before 'Change' arrives, it is not too late for My children who have ignored Our warnings to repent to turn to Us and be forgiven. Then the change that comes to them will benefit their lives."

Looking ahead, I saw that 'Change' went on for a very long distance. The further we walked, there appeared to be no end in sight. My Lord said: "This change that We are sending to Earth will be a long-lasting change and will impact the lives of My children for many years. Do not be afraid, because it will not affect you in a negative way—ever! For those who are truly Mine, 'Change' will bring them joy. Many will have the desires of their hearts fulfilled. Destinies will be accomplished easily as well as long forgotten dreams realized."

Justice Is Coming

For God will bring every deed into judgment, including every hidden thing, whether it is good or evil (Ecclesiastes 12:14).

Days later Jesus continued to talk with me about the wave of 'Change':

"Didn't We tell you that great change is coming to this world? It is beginning to break out personally and worldwide. Good changes are coming for My faithful few and terrible, terrifying, changes for the unrighteous masses. Individuals who have walked in sin—even secret sins—will have their sins exposed and their consequences will fall on them, until they repent. This change is called 'Justice.'

"Yes, My justice is coming forth to reward the faithful and deal justly with those who have escaped justice for many years. Glory will pour out on My faithful ones during this season of justice! I am a just God, and because of My justice, I must reward those who diligently serve and seek Me. My greatest reward is My glory pouring over My children.

"My glory and My just judgments will be displayed in this hour. They will walk hand in hand throughout this land. As each one repents and turns to Me, they will exchange their grave clothes and ashes for My beauty. My glory will not be withheld from anyone who turns from their sins and begin to love and serve Us."

He continued: "You will see My hand arise in this hour to rescue My children from he who is determined to steal, kill and destroy. Yes, this is the hour for true justice to be made manifest.

"Justice has been kept from descending from Heaven to the Earth, but now is the hour when My angel armies will win the battle for the soul of your nation. Justice will have its way in your courts! Truth will be established when justice arrives. Ears will be opened to hear, and eyes that were blinded by the spirit of deception will see clearly what they could not perceive.

"My glory will chase away wickedness that has had free rein in your land. It will capture the hearts that were once stony, cold, and insensitive to My presence. Instead of living for themselves, or for this world, they will run into My arms where My glory resides. The things of this world that captivated My children will grow strangely dim in their sight, when the light of My glory overshadows them! Who would settle for a counterfeit, when the real is easily accessible? I am going to make My glory attainable to all."

> *I will display my glory among the nations* (Ezekiel 39:2).

Positioned for Promotion

> *For the eyes of the Lord range throughout the earth to strengthen those whose hearts are fully committed to him* (2 Chronicles 16:9).

Again while sitting beside the Father and Jesus in the spirit, Father told me that He would pour His Spirit out on this land. Because of the few who love Him with all their heart, mind, and strength and because of His justice, He is going to answer their cries. To my delight, I heard Him laugh heartily. He explained that it makes Him extremely happy to see what He is going to do for and through us. In an instant, I saw a rain falling all over the land and suddenly a great bucket of water was thrown on me; Father and Jesus laughed even harder.

Father said: "For those who remain steadfastly Ours, a far greater amount of My presence, My glory, will be poured out on them, because I am just. Actually, it is those few who We will be pouring this deluge on. Everyone else will be getting the outpouring, or excess, that comes off them. They will be splashed with My glory, while My faithful lovers will be saturated with it, because I am just."

> *I will no longer hide my face from them, for I will pour out my spirit on the house of Israel, declares the sovereign Lord* (Ezekiel 39:29).

I heard Jesus say: "Just as your enemy has used people to advance his cause, by putting charismatic appeal on them, I will be doing the same in this hour. By My hand, people will be drawn to those I have chosen to advance My kingdom. There are those I am taking from the backside of the desert like I did Moses and touching with My hand of favor so they can set My children free from their slavery to sin and deception. I will do it, for I am God, and I do choose those who I determined to use. I do put kings and officials in their positions of authority, and take down those I have rejected.

"This is the hour, in the spirit realm, that I am promoting My Josephs and My Moseses, and demoting those who have misled My children. This will happen in the church and in the government. Those who the enemy has put into office shall be removed and replaced by those I have selected. You will see this happen in this hour and are already seeing it begin to come to pass. Years ago, prompted by My Spirit, you did declare a 'changing of the guard' over your nation and this world! I am performing My words that you declared. Many will be taken down and replaced. Know this; it is Me—your God and Father—who is doing this.

"I have seen the struggle My righteous few have been enduring because of the actions of sinful mankind, and I am coming to set the captives free from those who have oppressed them, lied to them, and have stolen their inheritance. No man will stop me! For I am God and sovereign over all! The battle is on; it is raging now. The enemy will be defeated in all arenas! Stand steadfast in faith, trusting that I will have the victory and that My will shall be done on Earth as it is in Heaven.

"Dagon (the Philistine's false god) is being taken down, for I will not share My glory with any other. My glory, pouring forth on your land and through My righteous ones, will chase the darkness away and bring forth a new dawn! The false idols My children have been bowing their knees before shall be exposed for what they truly are; they will all be rejected, and I will be exalted."

> *... By their fruit you will recognize them... Likewise every good tree bears good fruit, but a bad tree bears bad fruit... Every tree that does not bear good fruit is cut down and thrown into the fire* (Matthew 7:15–23).

Recompense Foretold

Days later while alone in the spirit, I heard: "All will see how We do bless and promote those who steadfastly serve Us. At the same time, all will see how We do punish those who deliberately attempt to destroy the lives of My children and rob them of their destinies and livelihoods. This is the hour of recompense! All will see that the rewards of the faithful are tremendous, while the punishment of the wicked will not be escaped. It will motivate many to avoid evil and seek righteousness.

"Your land will return to righteousness. Righteous rule shall be implemented once again, and righteousness will become the standard by which men are judged. Evading a lifestyle of righteousness will no longer be popular, nor will it be emulated by the masses, but the reverse will be true. Righteousness will be sought after by individuals and by groups as well. The delight of My children will be to find ways to please Us. No longer will it be popular to break the law—not Mine or man's. The righteous ones will be celebrated, while the unrighteous will be shunned.

"Herald this new season with glad hearts and great rejoicing, for the rewards of the righteous are many. The outpouring of My Spirit—My glory—on your land, and many other lands, will saturate all those who hunger and thirst for righteousness with My goodness. Grand celebrations, for righteousness sake, will breakout. Yes, that which I planned will happen. A great outpouring of the spirit of enjoyment for life is about to be released from Heaven to the nations. The dry, thirsty, forlorn ones will be satisfied and filled with Heaven's joy!

"Your land, and many other lands, have gone through a season of sorrow and loss. This was not My will, but because many of My children have been praying for My will to be done, so now I can implement My will.

"Yes, now is the hour of recompense. I will recompense My children for all the hours, and even years of sorrow and suffering they have endured at the hands of the enemy and those he has used to harm My children. The empty vats will be filled with blessings from on high, which will bring about a recompense of great joy!"

A Convocation of Righteousness Is Coming

Delight filled my heart as I heard my Lord tell me this wonderful promise: "Great joy, great rejoicing is coming to your land. A holy celebration—a convocation of righteousness—is breaking forth and spreading. Love for us, love for your nation and its leaders will be the by-product of this season of recompense and righteousness.

"A spirit of national patriotism that was stolen from your land is being restored. This recompense of patriotism is a manifestation of Our justice pouring forth on your land. This patriotism was purchased by the blood of many over the years. In hard fought wars, your land was soaked in the blood of patriots. We have heard the cries of their blood and are—in justice—responding by restoring a spirit of intense patriotism to your land. It shall never be stripped from it again.

"To love one's land is not idolatry, but it is a demonstration of gratitude to Me for giving this nation to you. National pride is being restored. This will inspire My children, and the citizens of this nation who live here, to live with excellence. Hard work, which built this great land, will once again be heralded as good and esteemed by all generations. Laziness and slothfulness will be disdained and rejected by the masses and will be seen as a path to poverty and lack."

Mindsets Will Change

"Great work ethics will be imparted to all. At creation, I worked hard for six days and rested on the seventh day. There are those who have turned the tables and promote working one day and resting for six. No longer will this mindset be accepted by the masses. This nation will get back to work. Your debt will be canceled and prosperity will reign. You will be known as a nation that lends and never borrows.

"I will drop mantles of excellence from Heaven to My children. There will be a striving for excellence: in government, in schools where education has suffered, in churches where the gospel has been watered down, in the workplace where instead of doing the least, all will put forth their best effort daily, in families where faith, unity, love and sacrifice for others will be imparted.

"Mindsets that promote compromise with evil values will be changed. New mindsets will cloak My children. Thoughts inspired by the God who created them in His image will be embraced. They will once again follow the God who worked for six days and rested on the seventh day. My values and ways will be followed, and your land will be blessed forever!

"Diligence in all arenas will be sought after and rewarded. No longer will those who used trickery and corrupt dealings to get ahead be emulated or followed. Those who raise the standard of integrity and hard work will receive the accolade of the public; their example will inspire many to do the same with their lives. Heroes and heroines will arise in your land that are worthy of honor and praise. Diligence will be esteemed and sought after once again. This value will be attained by those who seek it in their homes, businesses, churches and government.

"Law and order shall replace anarchy, lawlessness and injustice. The values your nation was founded and established on shall be restored in this wonderful season of recompense that I am releasing, in answer to My children's prayers."

> *...The righteous will inherit the land and dwell in it forever... He will exalt you to inherit the land; when the wicked are cut off you will see it* (Psalm 37:29, 34).

Chapter Twenty-Two

Days of Elijah and Elisha Revisited

Elijah was a man just like us. He prayed earnestly that it would not rain, and it did not rain on the land for three and half years. Again he prayed, and the heavens gave rain, and the earth produced its crops.

—James 5:17–18

Numerous times when I have met with Holy Spirit, I have heard Him declare that these are the days of Elijah. I know that when He continues to repeat something to me, I haven't understood all He wants me to know. With that in mind, I determined to get apart with Holy Spirit and see what He was attempting to reveal to me through the life and times of Elijah. What I learned, with His guidance, is a significant and encouraging word for us in this hour.

Almighty God summoned Elijah, a very powerful prophet, who lived in Gilead in Israel in 875 BC, to accomplish a difficult task. Elijah's God-ordained assignment was to directly confront and eliminate the ruling spirit over the nation of Israel—Jezebel. This ruling spirit, or regime, was seeking to erase God from the nation. Jezebel, or the spirit that controlled her, introduced all kinds of sexual sins to Israel. This ruling spirit promoted prosperity for a small percentage of people and oppressed the rest. Jezebel rejoiced over the killing of babies and offered them as a sacrifice to the false God they served, Baal. In our eyes it would appear to be impossible for Elijah to take down this regime, but as we know, with God all things are possible.

After a season of conflict with Ahab and Jezebel, Elijah prayed for a drought in Israel that lasted over three years. This enraged the king and queen who vowed to kill the prophet. At the end of the drought, God sent Elijah to meet with King Ahab. All the people of Israel and the prophets of Jezebel were assembled at the top of Mount Carmel. To everyone's amazement, Elijah proved to all the people of Israel who the one true God was.

At Elijah's instruction, King Ahab and Elijah each offered a bull on an altar. Ahab offered his bull to Baal, and on Elijah's altar, a bull was offered to his God. Elijah declared that the God who answered by consuming the sacrifice with fire would be declared the one true God. After Ahab and the priests of Baal cried out all day, Baal made no response; but after just one prayer, Elijah's God sent fire from Heaven that completely burned up the sacrifice!

Elijah commanded the people to worship and serve the one true God and return to Him. He also demanded that all the false prophets of Baal be brought down the mountain and be killed. Because of God's help, in one amazing event, Elijah restored Israel's faith in God and shut the mouth of the enemy that was deceiving the people through the false prophets of Jezebel and Baal.

Once the sacrifice was accepted by God and His children restored to Him, God sent rain, ending the three-year drought and famine that had ensued. Enraged by Elijah's actions, Jezebel threatened to kill him. Fearing for his life, Elijah ran far away.

Filled with fear and discouragement, Elijah asked God to take him home. Instead of answering his prayer and removing him from the frightening situation, God sent angels to feed and strengthen him and personally met with Elijah, his prophet, and told him to get back to work. Before starting his journey back, God commissioned Elijah to anoint Jehu as the next king over Israel and to anoint Elisha as Elijah's successor.

In obedience to God, Elijah anointed Jehu and Elisha. He continued serving God until a short time later when Father God sent a chariot of fire from Heaven to pick him up and bring him to his homeland, heaven, where he is enjoying his great reward in glory.

Both Elisha and Jehu were very successful in accomplishing the work God had given them to do. Elisha, the new prophet, inherited a double-portion anointing from Elijah and used it powerfully, while Jehu had Jezebel thrown from the top floor window of the palace to the ground below, where she died a terrible death.

The Days of Elijah Parallel the USA Now

While revisiting the Biblical account of the life and times of Elijah, I saw many similarities that are happening in our world and finally understood why Holy Spirit kept telling me that these are the days of Elijah.

We, too, in the USA, have evil spirits ruling over our land—Jezebel being one of them. Over 3000 years ago, this manipulating spirit ruled over Israel. Just as it demanded the sacrifice of babies then, it is once again demanding the blood sacrifice of innocent infants to be offered to the demon entity, Baal. Since Roe vs Wade was passed, over 60,000,000 innocent babies have been slaughtered. In addition, sexual immorality is not just encouraged, it is promoted. The prosperity of a few prominent people is celebrated, and at the same time, the masses are taxed and oppressed. Corruption in government is rampant and evident to all, while the citizens negatively affected by this exploitation feel helpless to change it.

I believe that we are entering a season where God is about to change all this injustice and rescue us, like He rescued the deceived people of Israel, and restore our land back to Him. Like He used Elijah, an ordinary man, He will once again use His prophets and those who live for Him to bring about this deliverance from wickedness. Because the enemy knows that the prophets have great power to destroy his wicked schemes, as they faithfully wield the sword of the word of God, the prophets are being persecuted, just as they were in the time of Elijah. In this hour, just as He defended Elijah, our God will arise, encourage His weary messengers, and send them back to their posts to fulfill His plans for and through them.

Recently, the Lord again reminded me:

"These are like the days of Elijah. While you study about the times of Elijah, don't focus on the persecution, the rise of wickedness and evil leaders of his day. Focus on the victory of My prophets and the prayer movement's success to dethrone and destroy the spirits of Ahab and Jezebel. Focus on the many signs and wonders, the massive miracles, the sovereign victories My children experienced, the restoration of faith in God—the true God—and the mass exodus of believers from Baal's camp.

"These are the same victories you will see occurring in answer to the prayers and prophetic decrees of My children. All saw how great the God of Israel was and how impotent the god Baal was; in this hour all will see how great the one true God is. I will demonstrate My glory, power and goodness for all to see. Just as I sent the fire to fall on Elijah's sacrifice, I will perform signs and wonders for all to see, in response to the prayers and decrees of My prophets who love and serve Me. Let your faith arise; expect miracles to happen when you pray, and just as Elijah saw My glory, so will you and your nation." (See 1 Kings 18 and 19.)

> *O Lord, God of Abraham, Isaac and Israel, let it be known today that you are God in Israel and that I am your servant and have done all these things at your command. Answer me, O Lord, answer me, so these people will know that you, O Lord, are God, and that you are turning their hearts back again* (1 Kings 18:36–37).

God's Modern-Day Jehu

Again, days later I heard Holy Spirit say: "These are the days of Elijah—days of great darkness and greater light. Yes, the light of My glory and goodness always snuffs out the darkness of evil. Jezebel knows her time has run out to rule over your land and is throwing a temper tantrum. Pay her no attention; just continue pressing forward in faith and in prayer. You will see her and her puppets soundly defeated.

"Just as Jehu took her out in Israel, My Jehu will conquer this wicked spirit again. She and her doctrines will be destroyed. Peace will be restored, as righteous rule is established in your land. Don't allow fear of the idle threats Jezebel is sending forth through her ambassadors paralyze you or cause discouragement to back you down. This is part of the wave of change I told you is coming."

> *Therefore the wicked will not stand in the judgment, nor sinners in the assembly of the righteous. For the Lord watches over the way of the righteous, but the way of*

> *the wicked will perish* (Psalm 1:5-6). (See 1 Kings 21; 2 Kings 9 and 10.)

Great changes are coming to our land that will probably be messy for a while—like the mess that comes from a tsunami when it hits. As these disruptive changes occur, we need to stay steadfastly close to Jesus and continue praying for the lost to be saved and for His will to be done. He will keep in perfect peace those who keep their thoughts fixed on Him. (See Isaiah 26:3.)

Stand Your Ground

> *Away from me, all you who do evil... All my enemies will be ashamed and dismayed; they will turn back in sudden disgrace* (Psalm 6:8,10).

Alone in His presence, Holy Spirit continued to teach me His ways:

"These are the days of Elijah—days of glory, miracles and days of persecution. Do not run in fear when your foe breathes threats at you, but instead pick up the weapons of your warfare, stand your ground and fight. Then you will see your foe retreat and run in fear; all that he stole, or attempted to steal, will be restored. Stand your ground and resist all of his attempts to frighten you into retreat. Don't ever give up in discouragement, but instead stand fast and fight like a mighty, valiant warrior in your King's army.

"Declare what I say and what I promise; don't ever declare what your foe threatens to do to you. If you speak his words, then you give him the right to do exactly what he has threatened to do to you. Instead, as you speak My words, advance and fight the good fight of faith; what he has threatened to do to you will fall on his head.

"I am gathering My end-time army in this hour. Those who walk in faith and have learned by My Spirit's guidance to defeat the foe, will be selected by My hand to join the ranks of the fearless ones.

"Again I say these are the days of Elijah and Elisha—days of great glory and multiplied miracles; days where the church will impact the government and the world."

While He spoke, I saw a vision of lots of diamonds falling like snow, as I walked with Jesus in the spirit: "These diamonds are a sign of what is coming—of great value and greatly desired will be those things We shower down on you and your nation. This is a sign from Heaven of the new atmosphere you will be walking, breathing and living in. It will be an atmosphere of love, acceptance, joy, health, miracles and great peace; it will be an atmosphere of My glory!"

Deception Will Be Exposed

He continued, "There are those who think they know Me and know My ways, but they have been deceived because a spirit of deception rules your land. Where truth once sat supreme, now many wholeheartedly embrace the lies the enemy shouts to them about others, themselves and Us.

"These are the days of Elijah and Elisha; days when those mentored by My prophets will pick up their mantles and faithfully execute My will, speak My word, pray and proclaim all My Spirit wants to proclaim and pray through them."

He exclaimed, "Multiplied miracles are coming to your land, because I do have a remnant that is ready to run to their assignments. This is the hour for the double portion, for the overflow of My glory. This land will dance and sing of My goodness and rejoice in the love of the God who has rescued them time and time again, because He is merciful and compassionate."

Just like Elijah had all the prophets of Baal executed so that their lying propaganda was stopped, in this hour, we will see the company of God's prophets take out the lying spirits that the enemy uses to promote his wicked agenda through. All this will be done quickly, using the anointed word of God, not with violence or hatred, but in a spirit of love. Prophetic decrees will go forth through God's mouthpieces. Lies will be exposed, the truth proclaimed and believed, and both unity and righteousness will be restored, while those who have deceived the masses will be taken down from their positions of influence..

> *...the knowledge of the secrets of the kingdom of God has been given to you, but to others I speak in parables...* (Luke 8:10).

Elisha—A Prophetic Picture of the End-Time Revival

One sunny morning, while sitting before the Lord in my prayer room, I heard, "What do you see, My friend?"

As I have grown accustomed to doing, I opened my spiritual eyes and looked into the spirit realm and saw an enormous ball of fire traveling quickly from Heaven to the Earth. This ball of fire reminded me of the chariot of fire that came to the Earth and picked up Elijah 3000 years ago.

The Lord explained what this startling vision meant:

"That same fire is coming to the Earth again. This time it will come and burn with an unquenchable fire all the chaff of mankind's sins. That fire—the fire of My glory—will simultaneously cleanse and purify as well as impart passion and fervent love for Me into My children.

"The fire of My great glory is being prepared. The more My children pray, the larger and deeper that ball of fire will grow. I use every good deed done out of love for Me to fuel that fire. Even the hands of time are being set in a forward motion, from the intensity of the devoted prayers of those who love Me." (See Revelation 5:8.)

> *I looked, and I saw the likeness of a throne of Sapphire above the expanse that was over the heads of the cherubim. The Lord said to the man clothed in linen, "Go in among the wheels beneath the cherubim. Fill your hands with burning coals from among the cherubim and scatter them over the city." And as I watched, he went in* (Ezekiel 10:1–2).

From my study of Scripture, I knew that before Elijah left for Heaven, Elisha, his friend and successor, asked him a very difficult thing. He was a hungry man. He saw what Elijah had: so much power, so many miracles performed at his beckoning. He wanted the same anointing his mentor possessed, but because of his hunger, he would not be satisfied with just that. He asked Elijah if he could have a double portion of his spirit, his anointing.

Elijah responded that he could not give that to him, but if he saw him leave the Earth, then God had granted his request and was giving him double the power. When Elijah left in the glorious chariot of fire, in utter amazement, Elisha saw him whisked away in glory. He had received what he hungered for—a double portion. (Elisha's story is found in 1 Kings 19:19–21; 2 Kings 2–2 Kings 9.)

After the Great Outpouring

> *And afterward, I will pour out my Spirit on all people. Your sons and daughters will prophesy, your old men will dream dreams, your young men will see visions. Even on my servants, both men and women, I will pour out my Spirit in those days* (Joel 2:28–29).

In this unforgettable prophetic encounter, I was shown that Elisha's ministry is a picture of the end-time revival. When this revival arrives, it will be the long-awaited time of the promised double-portion anointing, or the time of the latter rain. In the natural realm, the latter rain is the rain that comes after the crops have been sown in the spring, have matured through the long, hot summer months, and are awaiting their harvest. That is when the latter rains or the autumn rains fall. These are the drenching rains that bring in the harvest.

In the same way, God will pour out His Spirit on all flesh in order to bring in a great harvest of souls. For too long, *the showers have been withheld, and no spring rains have fallen* (Jeremiah 3:3). The hour is fast approaching for the heavens to open and for the autumn rains to fall.

Through the story of Elisha, the Lord revealed prophetically to me many wonderful events that we would be experiencing in the future.

After being taken to Heaven in a chariot of fire, Elijah's position as the prophet for his nation was given to Elisha; a new prophet led Israel. King Ahab died, and his son took over governing the nation. Moab, the chief enemy of God's people, was defeated. (See 2 Kings 2:1–15). These events are a prophetic picture foretelling that in the day of the great outpouring of the Holy Spirit, there will be dramatic changes in leadership in both the church and in the government.

In Second Kings 2:19–22, the bad water, which had made the land unproductive, was healed by the addition of salt. This water represents the word of God. Salt purifies and acts as a preservative. The work of the church, to proclaim the word of God, will be purified. Men's doctrines and ways have polluted the word and work of the Holy Spirit, but this will be purified during revival. Good, solid, Holy Spirit-led teachings will be present. In this hour of the great outpouring of the Holy Spirit, the church will be productive and bring in a great harvest of souls.

Even though persecution will come against the revival, it will be quickly thwarted by God. Second Kings 2:23–25 explains that forty-two young men who had mocked Elisha were mauled by two bears. These bears were sent by God to stop the abuse of His prophet. Through these events, the Holy Spirit revealed that God will deal swiftly with idolatry, blasphemy and contempt for Him and His servants. The church will have great authority over demons.

In Second Kings 3 we read that King Joram and King Jehoshaphat sought advice from the prophet, Elisha, who received a word of direction for them from God while a harpist played. As a result, their enemy was defeated. During this revival, spiritual leaders will affect the government. Godly prophets will be sought after for advice. Leaders will not seek after sorcerers or those working in the occult. Worship will bring an increase in the presence of God and in the gifts of the Holy Spirit. Prosperity will increase for many. The wealth of the world will be given to the just.

There will be a never ending supply of God's anointing, as seen in Second Kings 4. The widow of a prophet was in dire straits.

She was about to lose everything she had, but God intervened and told Elisha to multiply her oil. Once she sold the oil, she was able to pay off all her debts. Therefore it is clear that not only will we have God's powerful anointing, but, from that, the debts of God's children will be canceled; those enslaved in sin will be set free. Peace will be restored.

Resurrection power will be present during this great outpouring. In Second Kings 4:8–37, we read the dramatic events that surrounded the death of the Shunammite's son. This woman had blessed the prophet and even made a room for him to stay at in her home whenever he traveled though their town. Her beloved son died, and God miraculously raised him back to life through Elisha's prayers. In this revival, those dead, both spiritually and physically, will be restored by God's power. Those who have made room for God's presence in their lives and have blessed His representatives will have their prayers answered. Their lost loved ones will be raised to life as well.

A great famine had overtaken the land in Second Kings 4:38–41. Elisha asked his servants to make a pot of stew. Inadvertently, poisonous gourds were added to it. Elisha directed the servants to add a small amount of flour to the stew. It neutralized the poison in the pot. From this incident, the Holy Spirit revealed that death will be overcome; the agents of death will be neutralized. How wonderful! All sin, which brings death, will be exposed and rejected. It will be recognized as causing death. A small amount of the wheat of the Word of God will neutralize it. Very little effort will produce great miracles and bring life.

Through the events in Second Kings 4:42–44, the Holy Spirit revealed that famines will end. Hundreds were fed with just a small amount of bread. There will be more than enough both in the natural and the spiritual.

Furthermore, sin will be removed by the washing of the Spirit and the Word. Innocence, and our lost loved ones, will be restored, as depicted by the story of Naaman, the leper, who was healed while washing seven times in the Jordan. (See 2 Kings 5.)

The long list of the awesome benefits of the end-time revival continues as Elisha's story unfolds: Miracles will happen to assist in the building of God's kingdom. They will occur in every day events. At Elisha's command, an ax head that had accidently fallen into the river floated and was easily retrieved. (See 2 Kings 6:1–7.)

Spiritual eyes will be opened. People will see visions; faith will be increased; those who are enemies will be defeated by God miraculously. They will be converted and turned into friends. This is shown in Second Kings 6:8–23: The Aramaeans' army was sent to kill Elisha. The entire army was blinded by God's power, and Elisha, then, led them into a trap. He brought the blind Aramaean army before his king and instructed the king to show them compassion, to feed them and send them home. As a result of the mercy that was shown them, the Aramaeans became friends with Israel.

God has great things in store for us. He wants us to be prepared—to be alert and awake in this hour: For He is coming in power and in glory. He will fill our lives with good things.

Chapter Twenty-Three

TAKING OUR LAND BACK FOR GOD

Another angel, who had a golden censer, came and stood at the altar. He was given much incense to offer, with the prayers of all the saints, on the golden altar before the throne. The smoke of the incense, together with the prayers of the saints, went up before God from the angel's hand. Then the angel took the censer, filled it with fire from the altar, and hurled it on the earth; and there came peals of thunder, rumblings, flashes of lightning and an earthquake.

—REVELATION 8:3–5

On July 30, 2019,, long before the Coronavirus was loosed upon the world and the many violent, destructive riots erupted, the Lord gave me a prophetic word that foretold what was coming to the Earth.

While sitting on the familiar bench on the mountain of intimacy, where I often visited with Father and Jesus, I heard:

"There is a lot of unrest coming to the world. This will set the stage for a revival like none other. This unrest will touch many. It will cause the lukewarm to run to Us for the help they need. Yes, there will be riots in the streets of many nations—even your own. But in all this, I will remain seated on My throne, and My will shall be done on this Earth. Multitudes will seek My face, humble themselves, turn from their wicked ways and pray, and I will hear them and I will heal their land.

"Before this revival erupts, you will see this worldwide unrest. I am telling you this so you will not be discouraged or lose your faith in what I have told you is coming. This upheaval will put hunger and desperation in the hearts of My children. Just like when My people were enslaved in Egypt, it took the hand of a heavy, cruel task master for My children to cry out for deliverance. Suffering purifies hearts and motives far more than success and luxury does."

As He spoke, I understood that Father was not causing this civil unrest or intense suffering that was coming, but He was allowing it and would turn it around for great good.

Interrupting my thoughts, He continued, "Civil unrest is coming very soon, but fear not for I am on My throne and in control." While He spoke, I saw God's hand—huge and powerful—upon this world. As I watched this vision, Father taught me that it is His hand which keeps everything in order.

Then He lifted the top of His hand off the world just a little bit, and chaos reigned where there once was peace. He declared: "Only those who have My hand of favor on them will escape the chaos that is coming to this world. It will not last long, because many will run back to Me and multitudes that never knew Us will find Us. Evil will reign for a short time, but never over you or yours! The soul of your nation is at stake. Know this when you see and hear these events take place: I am a good Father who does discipline My children for their good and for the sake of their souls."

And we know that in all things God works for the good of those who love him, who have been called according to his purpose (Romans 8:28).

A Call to Mobilize the Troops

Jesus appeared to me in the spirit on September 6, 2019 and I heard a very important message. He was dressed in the same long, flowing, light blue garment He had on when I first saw Him, when I was seven years old. He was so strong and larger than life; His body was glorified. He invited me to come someplace very special with Him. I wondered if it was one of the places we had visited in the past, like the mountain of intimacy, the beach or the gardens in Heaven. He laughed heartily and took my left hand in His, and off we went together. We walked into glory.

Then out of nowhere appeared Holy Spirit on my right side. I never saw Holy Spirit so clearly before. He was dressed in a red and gold garment—representing His majesty and authority—and looking regal, like a warrior king. He too laughed heartily when He came next to me. Then, as we advanced in the spirit, I saw my Father sitting on His throne. All I could see was a brilliant white light pouring off of Him. As in the past, I could only see His form, and the form of my two Companions; no details of what They looked like was allowed for me to see. Jesus had taken me into the throne room to visit the Father with Holy Spirit. I ran into the Father's arms and just soaked in His loving acceptance.

Then He spoke to me; "A great war is coming to your land. This war will be different than what you expect. It will not be another nation invading yours, but it will be a war fought from within. Your foe is causing great dissension and strife—brother fighting against brother. His purpose is to stop the great revival from being birthed and advancing. He will not succeed. That is why We laugh. We know the beginning from the end. Far greater is My power than his power. I have those My Spirit will work through to fight the forces of darkness and to defeat the evil one." I knew this was why Holy Spirit was dressed in such regal, militant garments.

Then I heard the Father say: "Mobilize the troops, daughter. Holy Spirit will help you. Pick up the weapons of your warfare. I have trained My army well to use their most effective weapons—love and forgiveness. Through prayer, you will see those who hate all of that which stands for good and are blinded by deception turn to Me and embrace My ways. Teach My children what I have taught you. Show them how to pray with love, compassion and forgiveness for those who have sought to destroy, divide and demolish the nation from within. This is how the battle will be won: through prayers motivated by love, forgiveness and compassion. We rejoice because We know our power for good is far greater than the enemy's power for evil."

I realized that many of the trials I had endured from those who hated, rejected and mistreated me were used by my Father to teach me how to love my enemies, so they too could be set free.

Once again I heard: "Mobilize the troops, daughter, for the battle rages. Remember, you are on the winning side, and I will not be stopped from fulfilling My promise to pour My Spirit out on all flesh."

It has been over a year since Father spoke to me about this impending war. Recently, I have seen much turmoil, a terrible pandemic and civil unrest come upon our nation and the world. I know when the Father warns us and asks us to pray, it is because He wants us to apprehend His will and avert the plans of the enemy. God's will is to pour a spirit of enjoyment for life out on us and for peace, love and unity to flood our nation and the world. As His army continues to pray with love, forgiveness and faith, we will see this chaos, fighting, political corruption, the pandemic and the many riots stopped.

Jesus Has Come to Fight with Us

One Sunday morning in July 2020, while riding in the car on the way to church, I saw a magnificent vision of Jesus. He was dressed in His light blue flowing garment and was about a mile high; His feet rested on the Earth.

He told me: "I am coming to take back the Earth that I purchased through My death and resurrection that has been stolen by satan and his henchmen. I will scatter the enemy through the prayers and intersession of those who are Mine. I will set free those who have been held captive by his wickedness and establish them firmly in My kingdom."

He continued: "Don't focus on the things satan is doing and has done; but focus on the mighty God you serve, who is well able to save. I am the God who walked on the sea, who turned water into wine, who fed the multitudes by multiplying a few loaves of bread and a couple of fish, who raised the dead, who turned the storm-tossed raging waters into a calm waterway, and who healed and delivered all who came to Me. I did raise the dead, and once again, I will use My power, manifested through My bride, to raise the dead.

"Just a few prayers offered in love and with faith will bring great victories. Each battle My children fight, led by Holy Spirit and done in His strength, will be victorious."

Then He promised: "My children will be given special priority in this hour. All that has been stolen from them will be restored first: their reputations, their wealth, and their health, as well as their relationships that were destroyed. Watch and see, I will perform this word."

With determination He declared, "Like a snake, satan deceives My children, just like he deceived Adam and Eve. I am rolling up My sleeves, for the fight is on. Just a few prayers offered in love and with faith will bring great victories. The fight is on; My army is assembled. Miracles will happen! My glory will be poured forth!"

Aerial Tour of the USA

Listening intently, I was not disappointed when I heard Father say: "Pray prayers of faith for your nation, your president and this world, and you will see wonders to behold! In the past, I showed you My angels bringing the prayers of My people to My throne room; now look and see what We will show you today."

As the Father spoke this word to me, I remembered a few days earlier that the Lord had brought me in the spirit and showed me houses scattered all over the United States that were ablaze with fire. This fire was the fire of passion for God. I knew that His people were praying in these houses and that the angels were gathering the prayers and bringing them to the throne of God.

Now, once again in the spirit, I found myself flying between Father and Jesus over the world. I saw fires burning all over the land and lots of smoke pouring off these fires. The land was becoming covered in smoke.

Father explained:

"This smoke is the incense that is pouring off the intercessors' prayers. Gradually this incense is rising into the heavens. Just as in the natural, the particles in the smoke will eventually cause it to rain; the particles of love in these prayers will cause it to rain My Glory down on the Earth below. It is the love that motivates these prayers—love for Us and Our children—that will make the rain fall on your land. Inspire love in My children—for all; yes, for both friends and foe, and My Glory will fall.

"Prayers birthed without love and faith will not have the same effect. It is a waste of time to pray without love, forgiveness and faith. These prayers fall short and will not bear the fruit of My Glory. Revival fire will be the result of prayers that spread unity, love, forgiveness and faith. Peace like a river will flow wherever My Glory is poured forth on this land."

As Father said this, I saw rivers flowing all over the land, where the fires were burning brightly. The smoke that was pouring off each fire smelled like sweet perfume that touched the heart of God.

I also saw areas where there was no fire, no smoke and no rain. These regions looked like a desert, but, as I looked closer, I saw cities and even large cathedrals. Love was lacking; there were no prayers birthed in love going up to Heaven. Anger, violence, greed and sorrow was all I saw as I flew overhead. Father said, "Pray, My daughter, for fiery intercessors to rise all over this land, then My Glory will not escape any."

As we flew over Washington DC, I saw the White House ablaze with this spiritual fire, but many other government buildings were not. In fact, I saw people come out of these buildings with hoses and buckets of water. They ran to the White House and were trying to put out the fire by throwing insults, hatred, lies, bigotry and false accusations on the blazing fire. The closer some of these people got to this fire, the more the intense heat began to impact them and even stun some into accepting the truth.

Great Victories Are Coming

While in the spirit listening to Jesus, I saw myself walking between Father and Jesus, the peace of Their presence touched me deeply. The Father said to me; "Stay deeply connected with Us and no matter what happens, you will not lose your peace."

Father continued to talk to me about the days we were in:

"These are days of greatness! Yes, great victories, great doors opened, great powers and principalities dethroned, great medical breakthroughs, great inventions, great potential fulfilled, great glory and great revival. I do have an army that has assembled behind My Son, the Commander in Chief of Heaven's armies, and their exploits will be great. Just as David led the troops to battle, My Son will lead His troops to war. Using their powerful weapons, Holy Spirit has trained them to use, they will be more than victorious.

"Yes, as you see, the enemy knows this is an hour of greatness, too. He is attempting to bring great harm, great poverty, great loss of life and great defeat, but he will not succeed. In all his attacks, I will launch a counterattack that unmasks him and his schemes. His wickedness will repulse many, and these disenchanted ones will join the ranks of the army of God; this is the hour of the great unveiling."

Incredible peace filled my soul as I listened to my wonderful Father promise me that Jesus would help us gain many great victories and restore what we had lost through satan's relentless attacks. His glory would be arriving soon!

Chapter Twenty-Four

It's Harvest Time

Those who sow in tears will reap with songs of joy. He who goes out weeping, carrying seed to sow, will return with songs of joy, carrying sheaves with him.

—Psalm 126:5-6

One exceptionally sunny day while walking along a path in the spirit with Jesus, I was fascinated by what I saw. This path was unlike any I had ever walked upon. On both sides of the gently sloping trail were fruit trees of every kind: apple trees, cherry trees, blueberry bushes, strawberry patches, orange groves, grapefruit trees, to name a few. The sweet aroma of fruit filled the air. Chirping birds flew blissfully about from tree to tree. Laughing heartily, Jesus appeared to be as enthralled as I was by the richness of this place. Generously, He invited me to eat whatever I wanted. This fruit was the sweetest and juiciest I had ever tasted. The berries were quite large, and I wondered if they would be as flavorful as they looked. To my amazement, they were more delicious than any fruit I ever ate.

"This is the path of your life," Jesus explained. "These plants represent the seeds you have sown in service to Me and My Father. Every act of love, every kind deed and every sacrifice bear abundant fruit in My kingdom. Today I wanted you to enjoy the fruit of your labors. On the Earth, many times it is hard to see the byproduct of your labors. In My kingdom, all is plainly visible for everyone to see. I do reward those who diligently serve Me and show them the honor they deserve.

"All who walk this way know and see your extensive labor and the love that prompted it," my Friend declared. "Whoever partakes of the fruit is immediately reminded of the labor that produced it. I am glorified by the faithfulness of My friends, as they work on My behalf. I do reward those who diligently serve Me, and I make known their sacrifices. For I am a good God, fair in all My ways."

Enjoying the Delicious Fruit of Our Labors

"Today," He said, "I am bringing you to the place where you can enjoy the fruit of all your labors. On the Earth, many times My children work for Me and there appears to be no immediate good resulting from their diligence. But I tell you, in My kingdom, not one deed done for love of Me is lost, forgotten, or unproductive. No blight or insect infestation will harm this fruit or rob it of its splendor. I stand as a wall of fire protecting all My friends do for Me. Do not grow discouraged or lose heart when you do not see the good that your loving service has produced. Believe that I guard, nurture and water every seed of devotion you sow into My kingdom, and they will bear much fruit for Me and for you to enjoy."

As I ate the fruit, I began to recall people I had visited, prayed for, brought food or clothes to, and trips to nations where I had lovingly delivered the word of God. I even remembered times I had visited the sick and prayed for those dying of cancer. Children

I had served and befriended flashed before My mind. I heard, "I see, I know and I reward."

After walking a great distance through the fruit-laden path, I saw an area of freshly tilled soil. There were no weeds in it, just rich topsoil waiting for the new seeds of service to be sown in it. "Your work for Me is not complete," Jesus added calmly. "Remember, every act you do does not produce seed worthy to be sown here. Only those deeds, done for love of Me and led by My Spirit, are acceptable in My sight. Stay close to My Holy Spirit, and you will bear much fruit for My kingdom's sake."

His Burden Is Light

> *The harvest is plentiful but the workers are few. Ask the Lord of the harvest, therefore, to send out workers into his harvest field* (Matthew 9:37-38).

Continuing to look at this plot of land awaiting seeds, the Lord explained that there are times His children feel like they are done with the work of saving souls and caring for His people. Many have served Him well for years, but because of their age, gender, lack of formal training, or more commonly, because of the lack of receptivity by others of their ministry, they sit on the sidelines.

He said that there was much more work to be done and few willing to do it:

"All hands on deck. Now is not the hour to give in to discouragement. This parcel of land is so enormous, because there is much more work to be accomplished with My Spirit. I am not done with My children.

"The work ahead will not be as difficult as it was in earlier days. The soil has been tilled. The groundwork is laid. In seasons past, much time was spent getting the soil of people's hearts ready to hear My word. In this new season, hearts are prepared and many will readily and eagerly receive the seeds of life sown into them. I will touch many, and the touch of My love will immediately prepare them to not only hear and receive the word, but to begin to produce great fruit for My kingdom, too."

He showed me that because these seeds—or good deeds—were brought to Heaven by His angels, the enemy can't touch them. The enemy has no access to them, and they are well protected. What is being done in Heaven is also being done here on the Earth.

My wonderful Teacher explained that everything we need to be effective for Him will be provided to us. Through the outpouring of the Holy Spirit, He will empower each of us with the gifts needed to bring souls into His kingdom.

> *"Not by might, nor by power, but by my Spirit," says the Lord Almighty* (Zechariah 4:6).

Harvesters Come Forth

Gently He exclaimed: "Because of those who follow Us, all will rejoice, for there will be a great outpouring of the rain of My Spirit on your land. The overflow of My blessings will fall on all. My love, extended to everyone, will lead many to salvation."

> *...God's kindness leads you toward repentance...* (Romans 2:4).

He continued, "Call the harvesters forth. It is time for them to get ready to roll up their sleeves, for many who turn to Me will need instruction. This is not the hour to remain hidden away. I say: 'Come forth now, My bride, for the harvest is great!'"

The next day, back in the spirit, I saw Father and Jesus laughing heartily, sitting on either side of me, on Heaven's garden swing. Father explained:

"These are the days that We told you would be coming. They are just around the corner. These are the days that We told you We would be pouring out a spirit of enjoyment for life on your land. It makes us so happy to know that great joy will be poured out on Our children who love and serve Us, as well as those who will come to know, love and serve Us, too. After such a long season of suffering at the hands of your enemies, now We will turn your mourning into laughter. Great days of rejoicing are coming.

"Just as We did tell you to prepare for war, to assemble the troops, We tell you today to prepare for great rejoicing. Prepare your hearts to receive My best. Call the harvesters forth, because many who were lost shall be saved. We have great good in store for your land, and We will not be stopped. My will shall be done on Earth, because the army did gather and pray with faith, love and forgiveness. My will to bless all shall be done now!

> *Go rather to the lost sheep of Israel. As you go, preach this message: "The kingdom of heaven is near." Heal the sick, raise the dead, cleanse those who and he have leprosy, drive out demons. Freely you have received, freely give* (Matthew 10:6–8).

He Is Harvesting Our Deeds

Once again, my Lord spoke to me about the new season we were entering into: "Yes, this is a time and season of harvest. Just as a farmer goes out to bring in his crops, I am loosing My angels to bring in the harvest. Along with the good crop, those weeds that were sown by the enemy will be gathered, too. Evil shall be exposed, gathered and reaped.

"Many shall be rewarded for the good they have done, while at the same time, there will be those who reap punishment and misery. Fire—the fire of My wrath—will burn away the chaff of wickedness. Because I am just, I will express My gratitude and pleasure for those who have served Me well, and at the same time, punish those who have earned My sterner dealings. This is what is coming to your land now and will continue for many years. (See Matthew 13:24–30,36–43.)

He concluded our visit with this exhortation, "Those who refuse to repent shall know My wrath, but those who are Mine will know a season of great blessings!"

> *Whoever sows to please their flesh, from the flesh will reap destruction; whoever sows to please the spirit, from the spirit will reap eternal life* (Galatians 6:8).

Train the New Disciples

"I have called My bride to train My children," the Lord said as I saw myself, in a vision, gathering people out of the tsunami waters of revival and dragging them onto the shore. As they sat dripping wet, I stood before them and taught them all that I had learned about the spirit realm and about My Father.

These then went and took what they learned and gathered people out of the surging waters, sat them down and trained and taught them all that they learned. This was repeated over and over.

He explained the role of His bride in gathering in the harvest: "Duplicate yourself in others. Train people by your words and by your example. Hypocrisy will bear no fruit in this hour, but truth and integrity will. Just as My apostles learned well by My teaching and example, and they taught others, you do the same!"

The Masses Will Turn or Return

From the following encounter I learned to expect that a variety of people would be brought into His kingdom very soon:

"There are those who once followed Us, but now they don't. These shall learn quickly in this hour how much they need Us and how much better their lives were when We walked together. There are also those who never followed Us, but were far from Us. These too, will learn it is far better for them to be Our Friend than a friend of this world.

"The masses will turn or return in this hour. Prepare your heart and your mind to expect many more souls to be assigned to your care. I will assist you by My Spirit, and your joy will be full. These new ones will follow Us forever, for I am releasing a spirit of great perseverance to fall on each one, so your work on their behalf will not be in vain. Continue to pray and to believe that your God is with you, and I will answer all your prayers quickly.

To my great delight, He assured me what He would be doing during the coming harvest, if I just believe:

"In this hour of the great harvest, you will see many turn to Me like Paul did. I am discharging hosts of angels to Earth to bring forth Damascus Road encounters worldwide—as you believe! Over and above what you could think or imagine, We will do through you and for you, if you believe, My friend."

I believe that He will fulfill His promise to use us to gather in the wonderful harvest of souls because it is harvest time!

Chapter Twenty-Five

The Plight of Our Nation

The smoke of the incense, together with the prayers of the saints, went up before God from the angel's hand. Then the angel took the censer, filled it with fire from the altar, and hurled it on the earth....

—Revelation 8:4-5

Filled with concern for my nation, I hurriedly walked into my prayer room to meet with my Lord. As I drew close, He asked me what was troubling me. I explained, even though I knew He was already well aware of it, the terrible effects of the fires on the West Coast, the coronavirus that was killing so many people, the terrifying tornadoes that destroyed many lives and homes, the awful riots going on in our cities and the turning of our nation from godly values to liberal ideologies.

In answer to my pleas I heard, "Come with me, My friend. I have heard your cries for your country."

I entered the spirit realm, and together the Lord and I flew over the United States. The Lord showed me the fires raging throughout the states on the West Coast, the flooding rains in many regions, and the destruction of tornadoes throughout the Midwest. All, He explained, were the counterfeit of what God intends to do.

The coming antichrist will be a counterfeit of Christ ruling as King over the earth. The rains and floods are a counterfeit of the outpouring of His Spirit. The raging fires are the enemies counterfeit for God's spiritual fire that consumes the chaff of sin in the world and imparts passion for Him. The destructive winds of the tornadoes are the counterfeit sent by satan of the wind of the Holy Spirit that will breathe life and hope into our land.

The Lord said: "That is why you see visions of fires all over this land. At times those fires appear to be evil and destructive, and at other times, they are clearly the fires of revival. I must come soon and perform My works, for the enemy is pouring all his might down against My children. I will come and bring the real to destroy the counterfeit of his lies, the deception, the destruction, the diseases, the trauma, the plagues and the poverty. In My presence is the fullness of joy. My presence will exchange the sorrows and destruction of the enemy with the joys of My complete restoration."

For many months, I had seen visions of fires dotting the landscape of our nation and other nations, too. I wondered what these fires signified. At times when I looked into the spirit realm and saw these numerous fires, I felt like they were evil. At other times, I discerned that they represented something good. Now I understood. God's plan is to send the spiritual fire of His presence to the world. The enemy knows this and is attempting to subvert God's plan by sending natural fires to destroy our land.

Fires—A Warning Sign

In another encounter, while I sat with My Friend in the spirit on a high mountain overlooking the Earth, I observed that the United States had fires and catastrophic events taking place all over it. Immediately I prayed for Jesus to intervene and shorten the suffering: "Let there be repentance, changed hearts, and let God arise!"

Responding to my spontaneous prayer my Lord explained:

"So much suffering could be avoided if My people, who are called by My name, would turn from their wicked ways and pray. Many serious events have been curtailed because some have heard My cry to pray. There is much more to come upon this nation, if My people don't listen and repent and pray. Your enemy has loosed his henchmen to do their work of reaping the lost, before they turn from their sins to Me.

"Pray for the valiant few to arise and multiply throughout this land. Pray that they will assemble as one before Me, so I can act on their behalf. Just as the enemy has loosed his henchmen, I have given My command to My angels to release My glory and My presence to the Earth." (See 2 Chronicles 7:14.)

The following week, while in prayer, again I saw numerous fires scattered throughout the USA, but I also saw regions that were green, plush and free of danger. The River of Life flowed freely in these places.

The Lord explained what this vision meant:

"Daughter, keep your focus fixed on that which is good, beautiful and peaceful, and you will remain steady in the days ahead. I do not want you tossed about by every wave of the sea. I want you safe, secure and steady knowing and believing in your God who is with you. Keep your gaze fixed on Me.

"Read My Word and reread My words to you. Do not listen and become fixated on the words of those who speak of tragedies and dangers. Listen to My voice; I will speak the truth. I will warn you to move when necessary, to sell property, or to seek help when needed. So fear not. Being absorbed in Me does not leave you ill-prepared, but it does protect you from the curse of worry and the destructive properties of fear."

Another Call to Pray

Many months ago, alone with My Lord on the mountain of intimacy, I asked Jesus about a vision I had seen in the past. In many visions, I had seen fires burning all over the USA and was still troubled by their frequency and wondered if He was trying to reveal something that I was missing.

He answered with the following interpretation of those visions:

"These fires represent the plan the enemy has to destroy your nation. Your homeland is under a fierce attack from the powers of darkness. Just like when the fires broke out in your state recently, you relentlessly cried out for the heavens to open and pour down rain to squelch the fires.

"In the same way, I need intercessors to pray for spiritual rain. Few are praying, and your enemy is winning. That is why I have shown you the state of your nation. In truth, it is a place laden with fires. Pray, and I will open the windows of Heaven over your land. I will pour out My Spirit in such great measures that no fire will survive."

Then I looked over the mountain's edge and saw the USA. Fires raged, but people began gathering in small groups to pray for our country. Some prayed on their knees, others stood with their arms raised high, while a few danced and worshiped on behalf of their nation. I knew they caught the attention of their heavenly Father. He stopped everything and commanded His angels to pour the rain of Heaven on our land. As they did, all those kneeling and standing in deep intercession joined the dancers. A spirit of rejoicing fell on the entire nation. Every tribe and every people joined in the celebration declaring that our King reigns, and the enemy was defeated.

In a short time, the whole USA was covered with people worshiping Jesus. At the same time, the regions that were black and charred from the fires began to sprout new growth. Grass, plants, trees and fresh foliage grew and overtook the blackened mess left by the extinguished fires.

"This is what is coming, if you will believe," He said. "Yes, this is My perfect plan for your nation. Pray with eyes of faith and a heart filled with hope, and you will see the glory of your God arise with healing in His wings."

I know that I am seeing the fulfillment of this vision. God's people are arising!

Fresh Fire Is Coming

Sitting on top of His holy mountain, with my Lord beside me, I heard Him declare, "So few truly love Me and honor My Father. Look; what do you see?"

I looked out over the land below and saw just a few small fires burning here and there throughout the land.

My Lord explained: "Each fire represents a life truly dedicated to Me, a person on fire for Me and for My kingdom. Sadly, there are few My daughter. Most of My children are self-absorbed and passionately in love with the things of this world. Instead of being passionately in love with Me, in most cases, I am an afterthought or am not given a thought at all.

"Because of the prayers of the few who burn with love for Me and for My Father, by the power of the Holy Spirit in them, I am going to pour a fresh fire on the masses. I will use those who adore Me to help Me spread this fire. Contagious is the love they have in their hearts for Me. That contagion will spread like a wildfire. None will be exempt from being ignited with a deep, passionate love for Me and for My kingdom."

Then the Lord took a flaming torch and held it out to me. The fire that blazed on this torch was lit from the fire in the Lord's heart. He touched the flaming instrument to my chest. Instantly my heart was on fire with a deeper passion for my Friend.

Then He handed me the torch and said: "Now you go and do the same. As I have shared the love in My heart with you, you must go and share that love with all I send to you. That is one way that My friends will spread this fire through your nation and others. Trust Me to help you with the work of starting fires of love and passion for your God."

The Lord instructed me that if the fire on my torch dimmed, I was to touch it to my heart where His Spirit dwells, and it would burst back into flame. The Lord also explained that the torch represents the Word of God!

Before I left the spirit realm He declared, "It is your love for Me that inspires others to love Me like you do. Watch as all those about you run into My arms, because they see that you live there."

Blazing Fires Doused by Prayer

Months later I saw, blazing fires that dotted the landscape of the USA, as I peered into the spirit. To my relief, this time I saw many women, a few men, teens and children holding fire hoses and dousing the flames with streams of water.

The Lord declared: "The work has begun. My word is being released and is no longer being held back through ignorance, cowardice or fear of man. The day has come when My Spirit is being allowed free rein in many lives.

"This is just the beginning. In the days to come, you will see the masses rally to support My name and stand for My principles. Truth will be poured out like water on the fires of lies. Injustice will be exposed for what it is. Evil will no longer be able to masquerade as good. Murder will be accepted for what it is and no longer tolerated because of convenience or cost. Obscenity and vice will lose their appeal and will be rejected and even loathed as I loathe sin, for My heart and My thoughts will overtake the thoughts of men."

Chapter Twenty-Six

Worship and Prayer Will Bring Restoration

You turned my wailing into dancing; you removed my sackcloth and clothed me with joy, that my heart may sing to you and not be silent. O Lord my God. I will give you thanks forever.

—Psalm 30:11-12

The Lord came to me in the spirit and invited me to go and fly with Him over the United States. Immediately, I went deep in the spirit and flew over the region I was so concerned about. I saw the terrible effects of the raging fires in the West Coast of our nation and the regions flooded with unrelenting rain. Then to my amazement, I heard prayers ascending to Heaven. I could actually see these prayers leave the Earth and soar into the sky, beyond the realm of the stars.

In an instant, I found myself before the throne of the Father in Heaven. I was shocked at the unceasing loud noise I heard. I asked Father, who I could only see through a cloudy mist, how He could stand all the commotion. He just laughed heartily and told me that

He loved hearing the prayers of His children. Because there were so many prayers coming forth from the Earth for our land, for the Coronavirus to leave, and for our nation to be restored to godly values, He told me that, not only would He heal our land, but He would pour out His Spirit and begin the next great revival.

When all this happens we will know that no man or government did it; our God responded to the cries of His people.

Then I heard: "Let no man rob Me of My glory. For as King Herod came under My judgment for doing the same, so will those who hurl insults in My face by taking the credit for what I do."

Leaving the throne room with Jesus beside me, we resumed our flight over the USA. I saw multitudes downtrodden and oppressed. Jobless and destitute, they walked around with a heavy yoke on their shoulders. As we rose in the sky, I saw the glory of God rain down on the entire region. Sorrow was suddenly turned to joy; a great rejoicing ensued. Miracles, like gifts, were being showered down on the forlorn masses. I saw people singing, dancing and rejoicing. They were eagerly sharing the miraculous provision with those around them. Love permeated this once dreary scene.

I asked Jesus when these things would happen and He responded: "Let it be done according to your belief, for it is by faith that I am allowed to release My blessings. Believe and you will see even more than this. Believe I will do this; then I can do it! What you are seeing today is My perfect will for your nation. Believe that My will shall be done here, as it is in Heaven. My will is to bless, protect and defend My children. Believe that I am a good God, filled with love and tender mercy toward My children. Believe and then receive of My fullness!"

Eagerly I asked the Lord what else He wanted to show me. Immediately my spiritual eyes were opened, and I saw the USA, poor and unable to assist Third World countries with their terrible plight of poverty. Then we rose higher above the states, and I could see America reaching out, in great enthusiastic joy, to those held in the grip of dire poverty. We had more than enough to help all in need. As we gave, I saw angels bringing a great increase to our nation.

He declared, "That's what is coming. Do you believe My report or the report of men that have said that you are on the brink of bankruptcy and will no longer be able to offer aid to other nations? What and who do you believe? Nothing is impossible for Me to accomplish, if you would believe in Me."

His Cry for Our Help

One day while deep in prayer, I saw the face of Jesus. He asked me to look into His eyes. I saw a deep sorrow, not the twinkling joy I had seen in the past few months. He explained that no one knew the horrors that Hell holds for those the devil brings there. He told me that in the past He had shown me only a glimpse of both Heaven and Hell. To see what Hell was like in its totality would have been unbearable for me. Just in the same way that seeing all the glories that Heaven holds would have made it impossible to wait for my homecoming.

Baring His heart to me, He sorrowfully explained:

"There are so few who truly love Me. If there were more who were willing to lay their lives down for My kingdom's sake, many more would escape Hell and enter Heaven. The cost of being completely committed to Me is great, and few are willing to pay the price of total surrender. My sorrow arises from knowing that many are dragged to Hell daily; if My children truly followed Me, they could have escaped.

"I need vessels to pour My glory through. I need vessels to command demons to release souls. I need friends who are sold out for Me and who will put aside everything to speak My words and warn souls. I need those who are willing to go wherever and whenever I need them. I need friends who will believe in Me and My great power and who will trust Me to work through them.

"Pray, for the laborers are few. The harvest is ripe. The enemy is ready to reap his harvest, but My laborers are few, and the few I have are unwilling to pay the price necessary to save souls. Holiness is the price: complete, committed and total obedience for love of Me. To serve Me wholeheartedly like Caleb did is what I need. Then many will be saved, and My sorrow will be turned to joy unspeakable." (See Numbers 14:24.)

"When I look throughout the Earth, I seek to find those who remain faithful to Me. Where are those who stay devoted in the times of trial? Where are those who continue to keep their eyes fixed on Me when they are prospered? And where are those who still call Me Lord when they are disappointed or discouraged?"

He exclaimed: "There are those who love Me and remain faithful, no matter what, but they are few! In this hour, it is the faithful few that I will call out of their wilderness to advance My kingdom. Just as I stood back and watched Job endure his suffering and Daniel his persecution, I have been standing back and watching for those who will arise faithful and true."

The Future USA

I saw a gentle mist in the spirit realm which turned into a soft gentle rain. Then the rain intensified and gradually became a steady downpour. Then torrents of rain fell from the sky. I stood in the midst of this downpour, in this interactive vision, and was saturated through and through, but I loved it. Like a child, I laughed and drank in the delicious rain, while dancing with total abandon and delight.

"This is coming very soon, My friend," He said. "You are already feeling the mist and a few raindrops of My glory. My Spirit is being poured out on your land, as you asked. All will feel the effects; for your Father allows the rain to fall on the just, as well as the unjust. All will have the opportunity to turn fully to Me, and all will have the opportunity to be filled with My greatest blessing—My Spirit!"

Then I heard angels declare, "It's coming! It's coming" over and over like a jubilant herald announcing a great event.

He described, with great emotion, what the coming revival would look like:

"Some won't recognize Me, but most will, for nothing else can explain or duplicate My presence, My peace or My love. All will be transformed by My glory. From glory to glory, all will begin to resemble Me. My goodness will be embraced and emulated by most.

"Now it is the one who honors Me that stands out as different or odd. In that hour, it will be the one who doesn't bend his or her knee before Me that will stand out as odd or different.

"It is the great hunger of the few that is going to draw My presence to the Earth. Those few who withstood the jeers of the multitudes for love of Me have caught My attention, and I will come at their request to bless all mankind. I do love them, and I have heard their cries for mercy on the masses. Those few faithful ones have paid the price of devotion that a powerful revival requires. Unashamed, they have loved Me and stood fast as examples to all who looked on in disbelief."

Pray for Rain

> *As it was in the days of Noah, so it will be at the coming of the Son of Man* (Matthew 24:37).

My Lord concluded: "Yes, sin reigned over all the Earth in the days of Noah. Do not forget that in the days of Noah, I did open the windows of Heaven over the land. As the rain fell, evil was destroyed. From the rain-soaked Earth, a righteous remnant rose to take the land for Me. In this hour, I will open the windows of Heaven once again. I will send the spiritual rain of My Holy Spirit to wash away all evil. Blind eyes will be opened, and My glory will be revealed and accepted!"

He exclaimed emphatically, "Pray with faith for this spiritual rain to be poured out on your land!"

He has heard our cries! Restoration and rain are coming!!

While walking up a steep, stark mountain, I could hear water flowing from the height above. Wonder filled my heart; "Lord what am I hearing; where are you taking me today?" Those were just some of the questions I asked my Friend, as He led me forward in the spirit through this drought-laden land.

Then, as out of nowhere, the mountainside veered to the right, and I entered a new land. It was raining continually here. Though it appeared to be a natural rain, I knew it was the rain of His Spirit pouring down on this land. As far as I could see, plush, green grass, bountiful gardens of flowers, streams, rivers and lakes sprawled before me. (See Isaiah 60; 2 Chronicles 7:12–16.)

My Lord explained: "This is truly on its way, My child, for I am going to end the drought. Your land will be restored to its original intent: a land flowing with milk and honey; a land blessed by the hand of God; a place where My glory resides. I have heard the cries of My children for My presence to fill your land once again. Yes, I say once again, for your forefathers knew My glory and experienced the abundant outpouring of My love."

Great joy and faith filled my heart as I beheld this land—my land. The rain fell continually here, but instead of being wet by this rain, love, goodness, joy and tremendous blessings were what landed on everything and everyone. Rainbows dotted the landscape. This scene reminded me of what I had seen months earlier in Heaven.

As always my Friend answered my questioning thoughts:

"Yes, this is similar, but it is not Heaven. What you are seeing is a little bit of Heaven coming to the Earth, for wherever My presence is, Heaven resides. All the glories of Heaven will be at your disposal during this next great outpouring of My Spirit."

Looking past the horizon, I could see large flashes of light. It appeared as though bombs were exploding far away. I knew that in the future, terrifying events would happen in other nations, but it would not affect the USA once this revival arrives. Instead of our nation being impacted by these catastrophic events, we would impact others with our love, joy, peace, protection and provision.

Then I heard Him declare: "A place of refuge in the storms of life is what I have called your nation to be. The enemy has tried unsuccessfully to rob you of your destiny. What I declare cannot be stopped, and I say the USA will be a city of refuge for the world, by My power and not by the efforts of any man. Daughter, this is coming very soon. You will live to see it and will be blessed by the benefits of this great move of God."

His comforting words brought me great joy, "Everything you both need and desire will be provided during this outpouring of My love, grace, and power."

> *"Then this city will bring me renown, joy, praise and honor before all nations on earth that hear all the good things I do for it; they will be in awe and will tremble at the abundant prosperity and peace I provide for it.…For I will restore the fortunes of the land as they were before," says the Lord* (Jeremiah 33:9, 11).

A Place of Refuge

The Lord explained that those who come to our land seeking refuge during this time will be of a great benefit to us. Like Daniel and his three friends were to Babylon, they will bring their talent, character and abilities to our shores and greatly enhance our nation.

> *The Lord is good, a refuge in times of trouble* (Nahum 1:7).

The enemy has tried to abort God's plan to make us a city of refuge by bringing illegal aliens to our nation, which have robbed us of our resources and oppressed our citizens. Those who come will come legally and will enhance our society with their great wisdom and abilities (see Daniel 1:3–7). Then I asked the Lord when this would happen and He explained, "It has already begun."

As He spoke these words, I saw a mist that looked like a heavy fog, not quite a rain or drizzle, but such a deep mist fell—all it touched were saturated through and through. This thick mist approached the shores of the USA and traveled inland from the north, south, east and west. Canada appeared to be part of this outpouring, as well as segments of South America. Looking at that rolling mist come from the ocean, onto our shores, made me think of this Scripture:

> *You trample the sea with your horses, churning the great waters* (Habakkuk 3:15).

It was like He and His angels were riding across the oceans into our land, and the mist, the effects of the churning waters, accompanied them.

And then I asked, "When will the rain begin? When will your glory fall, Father?"

He responded, "Soon, My daughter, very soon. The deeper the hunger, the wider the thirst of My children for My Spirit, the sooner and the greater the deluge will be."

Then He spoke to me about those who have faithfully interceded for this nation by repenting and worshiping on behalf of those who won't:

"Those who have worshiped Me, have laid down a sacrifice of praise. Humbly each came before My throne of grace and mercy on behalf of others. This has pleased My heart, for love alone motivates hearts that cry out on behalf of those who don't reach out to Me. Love alone inspires so great a sacrifice, for My children don't benefit immediately, when they stand in the gap for others.

"But I tell you that in this hour, as each one cries out for others to be forgiven and blessed; I will come into their lives and bless them." He promised, "The seeds of sacrifice will reap an immediate return."

> *To him who overcomes, I will give the right to sit with me on my throne, just as I overcame and sat down with my Father on his throne. He who has an ear, let him hear what the Spirit says to the churches* (Revelation 4:21–22).

There Is Hope for You

> *God who began a good work in you will carry it on to completion until the day of Christ Jesus* (Philippians 1:6).

The hour is late, but it is not too late for individuals to turn to Jesus. Whatever happens on the Earth in the years to come, there is a hereafter. Heaven could be your home eternally, if you make a free choice to receive His forgiveness for your sins and embrace the salvation He purchased for you on Calvary. Faith in Him and in His love for you can change your life here on Earth now and will change your eternal destiny forever.

> *"Everyone who calls on the name of the Lord will be saved."* (Romans 10:13).

Do not miss the opportunity to embrace Him and know the comfort of being His. The wonders of His goodness and glory will be poured out soon, and He wants all of His children to receive His abundance now and forever in Heaven!

For all those that are not sure if your eternal home is in Heaven, below is a prayer that you may wish to pray, so that you can know of a certainty that you belong to Him:

> *Jesus, I believe that You are the Son of God and that You left Heaven to offer a sacrifice for my sins and the sins of this world. I am sorry for all the sins I have committed during my life. Please forgive me. I believe that You died on the cross to pay the full price for my sins, so I could be forgiven, and I accept the sacrifice You laid down on the cross for me personally. I believe that You rose from the dead, and with You I can live again in eternity. I give You my life and promise to follow You and embrace Your ways. Please come and live in my heart and fill me with Your Holy Spirit.*

If you chose to sincerely pray this prayer, you can be assured that no matter what comes upon the Earth in the years to come, He will take care of you forever—here and in Heaven.

In order to carry out the commitment you have made to follow Jesus, a few things would greatly benefit you. Get a Bible and read it daily. Talk with your new Friend who lives within you. He loves to listen and will speak to you; you will hear Him if you listen carefully. Find other Christians to spend time with. Finally, ask Him to lead you to a church where you can grow in His grace. Don't fear the future. It's in His hands!—and so are you!!

> *For God so loved the world that he gave his one and only Son, that whoever believes in him shall not perish*

but have eternal life. For God did not send his Son into the world to condemn the world, but to save the world through him (John 3:16-17).

ABOUT DONNA RIGNEY

For further information, you can contact Donna Rigney

through her email address:

hisheartinternational@yahoo.com

Donna's book relating her impacting and vivid visits to Heaven and Hell:

DIVINE ENCOUNTERS

has inspired many and is available through Amazon.com or other fine retailers.

It is also available as an e-book.

Visit Donna's website:

www.donnarigney.org